Are There Two
Americas?

Other Books in the Current Controversies Series

Are There Two Americas?

Caleb Bissinger, Book Editor

Published in 2018 by Greenhaven Publishing, LLC
353 3rd Avenue, Suite 255, New York, NY 10010

Copyright © 2018 by Greenhaven Publishing, LLC

First Edition

Articles in Greenhaven Publishing anthologies are often edited for length to meet page
requirements. In addition, original titles of these works are changed to clearly present
the main thesis and to explicitly indicate the author's opinion. Every effort is made to
ensure that Greenhaven Publishing accurately reflects the original intent of the authors.
Every effort has been made to trace the owners of the copyrighted material.

Cover image: Victor Moussa/Shutterstock.com; maps
adapted from Malachy666/Shutterstock.com.

Cataloging-in-Publication Data
Names: Bissinger, Caleb, editor.
Title: Are there two Americas? / edited by Caleb Bissinger.
Description: New York : Greenhaven Publishing, 2018. | Series: Current controversies
| Includes bibliographical references and index. | Audience: Grades 9-12.
Identifiers: LCCN ISBN 9781534502338 (library bound) | ISBN 9781534502390 (pbk.)
Subjects: LCSH: Equality--United States--Juvenile literature. | Segregation--United
States--Juvenile literature. | Discrimination--United States--Juvenile literature.
| Civil rights--United States--Juvenile literature. | Prejudices--United States--
Juvenile literature. | United States--Social conditions--Juvenile literature.
Classification: LCC HM821.A74 2018 | DDC 305.800973--dc23

Manufactured in the United States of America

Website: http://greenhavenpublishing.com

Contents

Chapter 1: Did Historical Fractures Sow the Seeds for a Divide in Contemporary America?

Richard White

The late nineteenth century was a period of massive change in
America as the nation reunified after the Civil War, expanded
west, grew more urban, and saw a surge in immigration and
industrialization.

**Yes: The nation is divided, and you can thank history
and geography**

David Morris

The Thirteenth Amendment ended slavery, but African Americans
faced great inequities throughout the twentieth century and today
confront racially biased voting restrictions and mass incarceration.

Brian Thiede, Steven Beda, Lillie Greiman, et al.

Rural areas are poorer than their urban counterparts and have slower
job growth, but they are also entrepreneurial.

Raza Rumi

The urban-rural divide had a decisive role in the 2016 presidential
election, as urban voters tended to support Hillary Clinton and rural
voters tended to support Donald Trump.

Chapter 2: Does Popular Culture Have the Power to Unite the Country?

Chapter 3: Do National Tragedies Bring the Country Together?

The aftermath of the 2016 attack in Orlando didn't bring the nation together. Instead, it led to bitter disagreement between people on either side of the political spectrum.

Chapter 4: Did the 2016 Presidential Election Divide America Beyond Repair?

No: The election may have been divisive, but the nation can still unite

Foreword

"Controversy" is a word that has an undeniably unpleasant connotation. It carries a definite negative charge. Controversy can spoil family gatherings, spread a chill around classroom and campus discussion, inflame public discourse, open raw civic wounds, and lead to the ouster of public officials. We often feel that controversy is almost akin to bad manners, a rude and shocking eruption of that which must not be spoken or thought of in polite, tightly guarded society. To avoid controversy, to quell controversy, is often seen as a public good, a victory for etiquette, perhaps even a moral or ethical imperative.

Yet the studious, deliberate avoidance of controversy is also a whitewashing, a denial, a death threat to democracy. It is a false sterilizing and sanitizing and superficial ordering of the messy, ragged, chaotic, at times ugly processes by which a healthy democracy identifies and confronts challenges, engages in passionate debate about appropriate approaches and solutions, and arrives at something like a consensus and a broadly accepted and supported way forward. Controversy is the megaphone, the speaker's corner, the public square through which the citizenry finds and uses its voice. Controversy is the life's blood of our democracy and absolutely essential to the vibrant health of our society.

Our present age is certainly no stranger to controversy. We are consumed by fierce debates about technology, privacy, political correctness, poverty, violence, crime and policing, guns, immigration, civil and human rights, terrorism, militarism, environmental protection, and gender and racial equality. Loudly competing voices are raised every day, shouting opposing opinions, putting forth competing agendas, and summoning starkly different visions of a utopian or dystopian future. Often these voices attempt to shout the others down; there is precious little listening and considering among the cacophonous din. Yet listening and considering, too, are essential to the health of a democracy. If controversy is democracy's lusty lifeblood, respectful listening and careful thought are its higher faculties, its brain, its conscience.

Current Controversies does not shy away from or attempt to hush the loudly competing voices. It seeks to provide readers with as wide and representative as possible a range of articulate voices on any given controversy of the day, separates each one out to allow it to be heard clearly and fairly, and encourages careful listening to each of these well-crafted, thoughtfully expressed opinions, supplied by some of today's leading academics, thinkers, analysts, politicians, policy makers, economists, activists, change agents, and advocates. Only after listening to a wide range of opinions on an issue, evaluating the strengths and weaknesses of each argument, assessing how well the facts and available evidence mesh with the stated opinions and conclusions, and thoughtfully and critically examining one's own beliefs and conscience can the reader begin to arrive at his or her own conclusions and articulate his or her own stance on the spotlighted controversy.

This process is facilitated and supported in each Current Controversies volume by an introduction and chapter overviews that provide readers with the essential context they need to begin engaging with the spotlighted controversies, with the debates surrounding them, and with their own perhaps shifting or nascent opinions on them. Chapters are organized around several key questions that are answered with diverse opinions representing all points on the political spectrum. In its content, organization, and methodology, readers are encouraged to determine the authors' point of view and purpose, interrogate and analyze the various arguments and their rhetoric and structure, evaluate the arguments' strengths and weaknesses, test their claims against available facts and evidence, judge the validity of the reasoning, and bring into clearer, sharper focus the reader's own beliefs and conclusions and how they may differ from or align with those in the collection or those of classmates.

Research has shown that reading comprehension skills improve dramatically when students are provided with compelling, intriguing, and relevant "discussable" texts. The subject matter of these collections could not be more compelling, intriguing, or urgently relevant to today's students and the world they are poised to inherit. The anthologized articles also provide the basis for stimulating, lively, and passionate classroom debates. Students who are compelled to anticipate objections to their own argument and identify the flaws in those of an opponent read more carefully, think more critically, and steep themselves in relevant context, facts, and information more thoroughly. In short, using discussable text of the kind provided by every single volume in the Current Controversies series encourages close reading, facilitates reading comprehension, fosters research, strengthens critical thinking, and greatly enlivens and energizes classroom discussion and participation. The entire learning process is deepened, extended, and strengthened.

If we are to foster a knowledgeable, responsible, active, and engaged citizenry, we must provide readers with the intellectual, interpretive, and critical-thinking tools and experience necessary to make sense of the world around them and of the all-important debates and arguments that inform it. We must encourage them not to run away from or attempt to quell controversy but to embrace it in a responsible, conscientious, and thoughtful way, to sharpen and strengthen their own informed opinions by listening to and critically analyzing those of others. This series encourages respectful engagement with and analysis of current controversies and competing opinions and fosters a resulting increase in the strength and rigor of one's own opinions and stances. As such, it helps readers assume their rightful place in the public square and provides them with the skills necessary to uphold their awesome responsibility—guaranteeing the continued and future health of a vital, vibrant, and free democracy.

Introduction

> "*Some countries are so large that the different populations which inhabit them have contradictory interests, although they are the subjects of the same Government, and they may thence be in a perpetual state of opposition.*"
>
> — *Alexis de Toqueville, political scientist*

One nation, indivisible, with liberty and justice for all…" Francis Bellamy, a thirty-six-year-old Baptist minister from Mount Morris, New York, wrote those words in 1892. Today, they are as permanent as granite, recited morning after morning, borne by memories from sea to shining sea. *One nation, indivisible.* Three words, profound and durable; true or not, they draw from a deep well of American idealism. One hundred and sixteen years before Bellamy, Benjamin Franklin, remarking on the Declaration of Independence, supposedly punned, "We must all hang together, or most assuredly we shall hang separately." The United States, from the very start, has prided itself on its solidarity. It resounds to the marrow.

And yet the history of the country is one of division and strife. The Founding Fathers feuded: was this to be a nation of rural farmers or urban strivers? Three years before the Civil War, Abraham Lincoln decreed: "A house divided against itself cannot stand. I believe this government cannot endure, permanently, half slave and half free. I do not expect the Union to be dissolved—I do not expect the house to fall—but I do expect it will cease to be divided." Women's suffrage, the civil rights movement, opposition to the Vietnam War, the fight for marriage equality—in such moments, citizens responded to a sundered society, one in which rights were withheld, equality denied, and beliefs tested.

At the 2004 Democratic National Convention, Barack Obama, then an Illinois state senator, said: "There is not a liberal America and a conservative America—there is the United States of America. There is not a Black America and a White America and Latino America and Asian America—there's the United States of America." But the United States of America often feels polarized, antagonistic, and bitter. It can seem as if binaries define us: rich or poor, urban or rural, Democrat or Republican, educated or uneducated. One wonders if discord is the nation's default mode. The novelist and essayist Jonathan Franzen put it this way:

> "[It is] fashionable … nowadays to say that there is no America anymore, there are only Americas; that the only things a black lesbian New Yorker and a Southern Baptist Georgian have in common are the English language and the federal income tax. The likelihood, however, is that both the New Yorker and the Georgian watch [*Late Night*] every night, both are struggling to find health insurance... both dream of fifteen minutes of fame."

Are there two Americas—one urban and the other rural; one black, the other white; one rich, the other poor? That's a question without an easy answer. The aim of this book, then, is to provide you with thoughtful, nuanced viewpoints on the historical, cultural, and political dimensions of American disunion and empower you to draw your own informed conclusions about the notion that this is a split nation.

In the texts that follow, you'll learn how we live today the legacies of the Industrial Revolution and the Civil War. You'll cross and recross the urban–rural divide. You'll encounter popular culture that has both united and divided the country. You'll have an opportunity to consider whether national tragedies bring people together or illuminate differences. And you'll weigh the ramifications of the recent presidential election.

In an episode of the television series *The West Wing*, a show that chronicles the inner workings of a fictional presidential administration, the character of the president says: "There are times when we're fifty states and there are times when we're one country, and have national needs. And the way I know this is that Florida didn't fight Germany in World War II or establish civil rights." This notion is worth considering as you progress through this volume. Perfect unity will never exist. That, after all, is why Thomas Jefferson called for a "more perfect union." He knew perfectibility was impossible, but striving for it essential. There will always be discord, dissent, and dramatic confrontations. So, too, there will be epochs of profound understanding. The national experiment is the testing of this duality, the coming together and breaking apart, the house divided and rebuilt.

CHAPTER 1

Did Historical Fractures Sow the Seeds for a Divide in Contemporary America?

Overview: The United States Has a Complex History of Discord and Upheaval

Richard White

Richard White is a professor of American history at Stanford University. His work focuses on the history of capitalism and the relationship between history and memory.

W hen in 1873 Mark Twain and Charles Dudley Warner entitled their co-authored novel *The Gilded Age*, they gave the late nineteenth century its popular name. The term reflected the combination of outward wealth and dazzle with inner corruption and poverty. Given the period's absence of powerful and charismatic presidents, its lack of a dominant central event, and its sometimes tawdry history, historians have often defined the period by negatives. They stress greed, scandals, and corruption of the Gilded Age.

Twain and Warner were not wrong about the era's corruption, but the years between 1877 and 1900 were also some of the most momentous and dynamic in American history. They set in motion developments that would shape the country for generations—the reunification of the South and North, the integration of four million newly freed African Americans, westward expansion, immigration, industrialization, urbanization. It was also a period of reform, in which many Americans sought to regulate corporations and shape the changes taking place all around them.

The End of Reconstruction

Reforms in the South seemed unlikely in 1877 when Congress resolved the previous autumn's disputed presidential election between Democrat Samuel Tilden and Republican Rutherford B. Hayes on the backs of the nation's freed blacks. A compromise

"The Rise of Industrial America, 1877-1900," by Richard White, The Gilder Lehrman Institute of American History. Reprinted by Permission.

gave Hayes the presidency in return for the end of Reconstruction and the removal of federal military support for the remaining biracial Republican governments that had emerged in the former Confederacy. With that agreement, Congress abandoned one of the greatest reforms in American history: the attempt to incorporate ex-slaves into the republic with all the rights and privileges of citizens.

The United States thus accepted a developing system of repression and segregation in the South that would take the name Jim Crow and persist for nearly a century. The freed people in the South found their choices largely confined to sharecropping and low-paying wage labor, especially as domestic servants. Although attempts at interracial politics would prove briefly successful in Virginia and North Carolina, African American efforts to preserve the citizenship and rights promised to black men in the Fourteenth and Fifteenth Amendments to the Constitution failed.

The West

Congress continued to pursue a version of reform in the West, however, as part of a Greater Reconstruction. The federal government sought to integrate the West into the country as a social and economic replica of the North. Land redistribution on a massive scale formed the centerpiece of reform. Through such measures as the Homestead and Railroad Acts of 1862, the government redistributed the vast majority of communal lands possessed by American Indian tribes to railroad corporations and white farmers.

To redistribute that land, the government had to subdue American Indians, and the winter of 1877 saw the culmination of the wars that had been raging on the Great Plains and elsewhere in the West since the end of the Civil War. Following the American defeat at the Battle of the Little Bighorn the previous fall, American soldiers drove the Lakota civil and spiritual leader Sitting Bull and his followers into Canada. They forced the war leader Crazy Horse to surrender and later killed him while he was held prisoner. Sitting Bull would eventually return to the United States, but he died in 1890 at the hands of the Indian police during the Wounded Knee crisis.

The defeat of the Lakotas and the utterly unnecessary Nez Perce War of 1877 ended the long era of Indian wars. There would be other small-scale conflicts in the West such as the Bannock War (1878) and the subjugation of the Apaches, which culminated with the surrender of Geronimo in 1886, but these were largely police actions. The slaughter of Lakota Ghost Dancers at Wounded Knee in 1890 did bring a major mobilization of American troops, but it was a kind of coda to the American conquest since the federal government had already effectively extended its power from the Atlantic to the Pacific.

The treaty system had officially ended in 1871, but Americans continued to negotiate agreements with the Indians. The goal of these agreements, and American land policy in general, was to create millions of new farms and ranches across the West. Not satisfied with already ceded lands, reformers—the so-called "Friends of the Indians" whose champion in Congress was Senator Henry Dawes—sought to divide reservations into individual farms for Indians and then open up most or all of the remaining land to whites. The Dawes Act of 1887 became their major tool, but the work of the Dawes Commission in 1893 extended allotment to the Creeks, Cherokees, Seminoles, Chickasaws, and Choctaws in Indian Territory, which became the core of the state of Oklahoma. Land allotment joined with the establishment of Indian schools and the suppression of native religions in a sweeping attempt to individualize Indians and integrate them one by one into American society. The policy would fail miserably. Indian population declined precipitously; the tribes lost much of their remaining land, and Indians became the poorest group in American society.

Immigration

Between 1877 and 1900 immigrants prompted much more concern among native-born white Americans than did either black people or Indian peoples. During these years there was a net immigration of approximately 7,348,000 people into the United States. During roughly the same period, the population of the country increased by about 27 million people, from about 49 million in 1880 to 76 million in 1900. Before 1880 the immigrants came largely from Western Europe and China. Taking the period between 1860 and 1900 as a whole, Germans comprised 28 percent of American immigrants; the British comprised 18 percent, the Irish 15 percent, and Scandinavians 11 percent. Together they made up 72 percent of the total immigration. At the end of the century, the so-called "New Immigration" signaled the rise of southern and eastern Europe as the source of most immigrants to America. The influx worried many native-born Americans who still thought of the United States as a white Protestant republic. Many of the new immigrants did not, in the racial classifications of the day, count as white. As the century wore on, they were increasingly Catholic and Jewish.

Immigrants entered every section of the country in large numbers except for the South. They settled in northeastern and midwestern cities and on western and midwestern farms. The Pacific and mountain West contained the highest percentage of immigrants of any region in 1880 and 1890.

The immigrants forged networks that shaped how and where they migrated and the kinds of communities they established. Chain migrations linked migrants to prior migrants. Early arrivals wrote home to bring family, friends, and neighbors to the United States. Over large swaths of Minnesota, the Dakotas, and elsewhere German was the primary language of daily life. Tensions between immigrants and the native born over the language to be spoken in public schools, Sunday closures of businesses (sabbatarianism), and temperance reform often put cultural issues and practices at the center of local and state politics.

Taken together, immigration and the end of Reconstruction triggered an anti-democratic movement to restrict access to the ballot box. By the 1870s proponents of restricting suffrage, having defeated an early push for women's suffrage, were calling democracy a mistake. They advocated restrictions on voting as a way to check corruption, elevate political culture, and marginalize those—they had in mind immigrants and blacks—whom they thought incapable of meeting the obligations of republican politics. They sought political changes that would make it far more difficult for the poor and immigrants to vote. Over time, through poll taxes, residence requirements, literacy requirements, and more, they would succeed. The mass politics and high voting rates characteristic of late nineteenth-century America would not outlive the era.

Attempts to restrict suffrage were part of a strong political and social backlash against immigrants that developed over the course of the century. The United States welcomed immigrants because they were essential to its growing economy, but nativists opposed immigrants as antithetical to American culture and society. They thought of immigrants as exotic and inassimilable. In certain situations, however, nativists had allies who were immigrants or the children of immigrants. Workers, both immigrant and native born, often feared that corporations were using contract labor—workers recruited abroad at lower wages than those paid American workers—to undermine American working conditions and the American family, which they defined as a working man whose wife maintained the home. They opposed certain kinds of immigration. One of the forgotten reforms of the period, the Foran Act of 1885, outlawed contract labor, but the law proved difficult to enforce.

Alliances of some native-born Americans with some immigrants against other immigrants proved most effective in the case of the Chinese. Roughly 180,000 Chinese immigrated to the United States between 1849 and 1882, and they became the personification of both the inassimilable immigrant and the contract worker. Although the Chinese came as free laborers, they were often branded as coolies: abject semi-slaves, whose low standard of living allowed them to thrive on wages that could not support white families.

Racists had previously claimed that superior Anglo-Saxons would inevitably replace "inferior" races. But in the West, while

Sinophobes saw the Chinese as exotic and inferior, they also thought the Chinese would triumph over the supposedly superior white men because they were efficient workers. Immigrants and the native born formed mobs that attacked the Chinese at Rock Springs, Wyoming, in 1885 and expelled them from Tacoma, Washington, in 1885 and Seattle in 1886. Congress passed ten-year restrictions on Chinese immigration in 1882 and 1892 and a permanent exclusion act in 1902. Late in the nineteenth century, those who opposed immigration from Italy, Hungary, and elsewhere compared those groups to the Chinese.

Some immigrants could wrap themselves in the mantle of Americanism if they were "white" and Protestant. Protestant immigrants, particularly Scandinavians and Scots-Irish, joined the American Protective Association in 1887 to restrict Catholic immigration as it rode a larger wave of anti-Catholicism that swept over the country. Aimed initially at Irish and Catholic schools, anti-Catholicism increased its range as new Catholic immigrants began to arrive.

Agricultural, Commercial and Industrial Development

Although not all of them intended to stay, most immigrants came to the United States for economic opportunity. Cheap land and relatively high wages, compared to their home countries, were available regardless of citizenship. The Homestead Act did not require that settlers filing for land be American citizens, and the railroads not only sold their land grants cheaply, they advertised widely in Europe.

The results of this distribution of fertile and largely accessible land were astonishing. Everything in the late nineteenth century seemed to move faster than ever before. Americans brought more land under cultivation between 1870 and 1900 (225 million acres) than they had since the English first appeared at Jamestown in 1607 (189 million acres). Farmers abandoned small, worn-out farms in the East and developed new, larger, and more fertile farms in the

Midwest and West. They developed so much land because they farmed extensively, not intensively. In terms of yields per acre, American farmers ranked far below Europe. Maintaining fertility demanded labor, which was precisely what American farmers were bent on reducing. They invested not in labor but in technology, particularly improved plows, reapers, and threshers. With westward expansion onto the prairies, a single family with a reaper could increase acreage and thus production without large amounts of hired labor. Arable free lands grew scarcer during the 1880s, forcing more and more land seekers west into arid lands beyond the 98th meridian. In many years these lands lacked adequate rainfall to produce crops. "In God we trusted, in Kansas we busted" written on the side of a wagon cover by a family abandoning its homestead summed up the dangers of going too far out onto the semi-arid and arid plains.

The expansion of agricultural lands led to what superficially seems a paradox: the more farmers there were—and the more productive farmers became—the smaller was agriculture's share of the economy. Farmers had the largest share of the dollar value of American economic output until 1880 when commerce's 29 percent of the gross national product edged out their 28 percent. In 1890 manufacturing and mining at 30 percent share of the GNP both exceeded agriculture's 19 percent share. During the same period, the percentage of workers employed in agriculture fell. A majority of the nation's workers were farmers or farm laborers in 1860, but by 1900 the figure had declined to 40 percent.

Such statistics seemed to reflect a decline in the importance of farming, but in fact, they reflected its significance and efficiency. Farmers produced more than the country could consume with smaller and smaller percentages of its available labor. They exported the excess, and the children of farmers migrated to cities and towns. Where at the beginning of the century exports composed about 10 percent of farm income, they amounted to between 20 and 25 percent by the end of the century. What farmers sold abroad translated into savings and consumption at home that fueled the nation's industry. Migration from rural to urban areas dwarfed both foreign migration and westward migration. American agricultural productivity allowed it to remain the world's greatest agricultural economy while it became the world's largest industrial producer.

The rise of industrial America, the dominance of wage labor, and the growth of cities represented perhaps the greatest changes of the period. Few Americans at the end of the Civil War had anticipated the rapid rise of American industry. For the first time in the nation's history, wage earners had come to outnumber the self-employed, and by the 1880s these wage earners were becoming employees of larger and larger corporations. As the Massachusetts Bureau of Statistics and Labor declared in 1873, wage labor was universal: "a system more widely diffused than any form of religion, or of government, or indeed, of any language."[1]

Skilled workers proved remarkably successful at maintaining their position through the 1880s, but they had to fight to do so. The relatively high wages for skilled workers led employers to seek ways to replace skilled with unskilled or semi-skilled workers. Mechanization provided the best tactic for deskilling work and lowering wages. Many of the bitterest strikes of the period were attempts to control working rules and to maintain rather than raise wages. Beginning with the Great Railroad Strike of 1877, through the Great Upheaval of 1886 that culminated in the slaughter at Haymarket Square, then through the Homestead Strike (1892), Pullman Strike (1894), and more, the largest confrontations often involved violence and the intervention by state or federal governments to repress the strikes.

Railroads

Many of these strikes involved the railroads; the whole economy seemed to revolve around the railroads. At the end of the 1870s the railroads renewed their expansion. With a brief break in the 1880s, expansion continued at a reckless pace until 1890. At the end of 1890 more than 20 percent of the 161,000 miles of railroad in the United States had been constructed in the previous four years. By the end of the century the railroad corporations rivaled the United States government in size. In 1891 the Pennsylvania Railroad had 110,000 employees, almost three times the number of men in all the armed forces of the United States. Its capitalization of $842 million was only $150 million less than the national debt. Nationally, 418,957 people worked for railroads in 1880 and nearly 800,000 in 1890: about 3 percent of the entire work force of the nation. By 1900 roughly one-sixth of all capital investments in United States were in the railroads.

The railroads powered the industrial economy. They consumed the majority of iron and steel produced in the United States before 1890. As late as 1882, steel rails accounted for 90 percent of the steel production in the United States. They were the nation's largest consumer of lumber and a major consumer of coal. They also distributed these commodities across the country.

At times, however, railroads threatened to haul the American economy into the abyss. Rail corporations overbuilt, borrowed recklessly, and were often atrociously managed. They ricocheted wildly between rate wars and the creation of pools to fix prices, and they encouraged other industries to follow. Wheat, silver, timber, cattle, and other commodities flooded the market, sent prices tumbling, and dragged many producers into bankruptcy. The signal of every economic collapse in the late nineteenth century was the descent of railroads and the banks associated with them into receivership.

The Economy

The railroads were typical of the economic contradictions of the era. Over the period as a whole, American industry advanced rapidly. By 1900 the United States had one half the world's manufacturing capacity. At the end of the century, it had overtaken Great Britain both in iron and steel production and in coal production. The United States made such great gains because it was the fastest runner in a relatively slow race. The entire period from 1873 to the turn of the century became known as the Long Depression in western Europe. The United States grew faster than European economies, although no faster than nations with similar British colonial backgrounds—Australia and Canada. It actually grew more slowly than Argentina. None of these economies, however, were remotely as large.

The growth was not even. Periods of prosperity alternated with deep downturns in a boom/bust pattern. The economy came out of the depression following the Panic of 1873 at the end of that decade, lurched into a short, sharp depression in 1882–1883, and then fell into a much more severe depression from 1893 to 1897. Until the 1930s this was known as the Great Depression.

Such fluctuations in the American economy were linked to the larger world economy. Important sectors of the American economy globalized, putting American businesses and farmers in competition with other places in the world. One result was a steady downward pressure on prices. The Republican policy of maintaining tariff protection for American industry mitigated deflation on the domestic market, but the return to the gold standard with the Resumption Act of 1875, which later became a major political issue, created compensatory deflationary pressure that contributed to the general decline in prices. This benefitted workers only as long as they were able to maintain their wages.

Economic changes manifested themselves in rates of immigration (which rose during good times and declined during bad), urbanization, types of work, family organization, and more. Social and cultural patterns, in turn, affected the economy by determining who held certain jobs, how those jobs were valued, and where and how work took place. The cumulative effects of these changes were staggering, and many Americans worried that immigration, urbanization, wage labor, and the rise of large corporations undermined values that they thought defined the country itself.

Social Change

The Civil War had seemed to secure the triumph of a world of small producers and the values of free labor, individualism, and contract freedom. Many Americans desperately wanted to believe that those values survived and still ensured success within the new industrial society. Sometimes they attached the old values to new theories. Herbert Spencer, the British writer and philosopher, had many American disciples, of whom William Graham Sumner of Yale was probably the most prominent. Spencer and his disciples tried to understand human social change in terms of Darwinian evolution, utterly obfuscating the mechanisms of biological evolution in the process.

Other Americans simply tried to portray the new economy as essentially the same as the old. They believed that individual enterprise, hard work, and free competition in open markets still guaranteed success to those willing to work hard. An evolving mass print culture of cheap newspapers, magazines, and dime novels offered proselytizers of the old values new forms of communication. Horatio Alger, whose publishing career extended from the end of the Civil War to the end of the century, wrote juvenile novels that reconciled the new economy with the old values of individualism. In his novels, an individual's fate was still in his hands.

Politics

Many other Americans did not think so. They formed a diffuse reform movement contemporaries referred to as antimonopolism. Antimonopolists, including farmers, small businessmen, and workers in the Knights of Labor and other organizations, agreed on the problem, but often differed on the solution. They lamented the rise of large corporations, which to them were synonymous with monopoly. They worried about the dependence on wage labor, the growth of unemployment, particularly during the frequent panics and depressions, the proliferation of tramps as the poor who wandered in search of work were known, and the decline of individual independence. In the 1870s Walt Whitman lamented the human casualties of the new economy. "If the United States, like the countries of the Old World, are also to grow vast crops of poor, desperate, dissatisfied, nomadic, miserably-waged populations such as we see looming upon us of late years—steadily, even if slowly, eating into us like a cancer of lungs or stomach—then our republican experiment, notwithstanding all its surface successes, is at heart an unhealthy failure."[2]

Antimonopolists agreed that the purpose of a republican economy was to sustain independent and prosperous republican citizens, but how to restore the economy to that condition was the problem. Some, probably a majority in the 1870s, sought government intervention to restore competition. Others, who grew in numbers in the 1880s and 1890s, accepted the inevitability of large corporations but desired that they be more tightly regulated. By the 1890s, the Populists, an antimonopolist third party centered on the South and West, advocated government ownership of the railroads and the telegraphs.

In many ways the antimonopolists were successful. They comprised large factions within both the Democratic and Republican Parties and created new third parties from the Greenbackers (1874–1884) to the Populists of the 1890s. In 1896, the climactic election of the period pitted the antimonopolist William Jennings Bryan against the Republican William McKinley. Bryan lost, but many of the reforms antimonopolists advocated would be enacted over the next twenty years.

Many others were already in place. The inevitable compromises involved in passing legislation left a contradictory reform legacy. Some measures sought to restore competition by breaking up trusts or holding companies while others accepted the existence of large corporations but enforced regulations to restrain them. The Sherman Anti-Trust Act of 1890 initiated a movement to break up the largest trusts. State railroad commissions, the most effective of which were in Iowa and Texas, and the Interstate Commerce Commission created in 1887 represented attempts to regulate corporations.

Symbols of Their Age

Certain people became better known and better remembered than the presidents of the period because they came to represent both the economy itself and people's ideological views of it. Thomas Edison emerged as perhaps the most admired American of the age because he seemed to represent the triumph of individualism in an industrial economy. He built his famous lab at Menlo Park, New Jersey, in 1876. The public regarded Edison as the "wizard of Menlo Park," but it was ironically the lab—a cooperative enterprise—that produced the inventions from a workable electric light to the phonograph and more. And when in 1890 Edison merged his lab and other businesses into General Electric, the man who was a symbol of economic individualism became the head of a large corporation. That the corporate form captured Edison was not surprising because large corporations that first arose with the railroads before the Civil War were coming to dominate the American economy during the Great Merger movement of the 1890s.

John D. Rockefeller symbolized the darker view of the economy. His Standard Oil became the best-known and the best-hated corporation of the day. Rockefeller ruthlessly consolidated a competitive oil industry, absorbing rivals or driving them out of business. He was unapologetic, and he had only disdain for those who still thought of the economy as depending on individualism and competition. Organization and consolidation was the future. "The day of the combination is here to stay," he proclaimed. "Individualism has gone never to return."[3]

What was also gone was the United States as a purely continental nation. In many ways, the American acquisition of an overseas empire was a continuation of its continental expansion at the expense of American Indian peoples. But with the annexation of Hawaii (1898) and the subsequent annexation of the Philippines and Puerto Rico following the Spanish American War (1898), the United States extended its military and governmental reach beyond

its continental boundaries. The war, like so many things, marked
the vast changes that took place in a neglected era.

Notes

1. Quoted in Amy Dru Stanley, *From Bondage to Contract: Wage Labor, Marriage, and the Market in the Age of Slave Emancipation* (New York: Cambridge University Press, 1998), 62.

2. Walt Whitman, *Specimen Days and Collect* (Philadelphia: David McKay, 1883), 330.

3. Allan Nevins, *John D. Rockefeller* [1959], 1:622.

The Divisive Legacy of the Civil War Lingers On

David Morris is cofounder of the Institute for Local Self-Reliance, which works to empower regions and communities to create bottom up change.

*T*he film Lincoln *ends after the Amendment that ended slavery throughout the nation passed. But for blacks, earning the rights of citizenship was to prove a much more protracted war.*

Lincoln is a magnificent movie. But as I left the theatre, to echo Paul Harvey, the late radio commentator, I wanted to know "the rest of the story."

The movie begins in January 1865, exactly 2 years after Lincoln issued the Emancipation Proclamation, declaring slaves of the Confederate States "thenceforward and forever free. "

As Lincoln himself told Secretary of the Navy Gideon Welles issuing the Proclamation was a "military necessity. We must free the slaves or be ourselves subdued." Indeed, Lincoln wanted to issue the Proclamation in July 1862 but Secretary of State William Seward cautioned that the series of military defeats suffered by the Union army that year would lead many to view such a move simply as an act of desperation. The victory at Antietam in September gave Lincoln the opportunity he needed.

The Emancipation Proclamation helped the Union immeasurably. It converted a war to preserve the union into a war of liberation, a change that gained widespread support in key European nations. And by rescinding a 1792 ban on blacks serving in the armed forces, the Proclamation solved the increasingly pressing personnel needs of the Union Army in the face of

"The South Has Been at Civil War for 150 Years," by David Morris, On the Commons, December 10, 2012. http://www.alternet.org/culture/south-has-been-civil-war-150-years. Licensed Under CC BY 3.0 Unported.

a declining number of white volunteers. During the war nearly 200,000 blacks, most of them ex-slaves joined the Union Army, giving the North additional manpower needed to win the war. As historian James M. McPherson writes, "The proclamation officially turned the Union army into an army of liberation…And by authorizing the enlistment of freed slaves into the army, the final proclamation went a long step toward creating that army of liberation."

Abolitionists viewed arming ex-slaves as a major step toward giving them equality. Frederick Douglass urged blacks to join the army for this reason. "Once let the black man get upon his person the brass letter, U.S., let him get an eagle on his button, and a musket on his shoulder and bullets in his pocket, there is no power on earth that can deny that he has earned the right to citizenship."

The movie focuses on one month—January 1865—and the Congressional vote on the 13th Amendment to the U.S. Constitution. Indeed, it could have been subtitled, "How a bill becomes a law." The film ends with triumphant celebrations by whites and blacks after the Amendment that ended slavery throughout the nation passed by the razor thin margin of two votes. But for blacks, earning the rights of citizenship was to prove a much more protracted affair.

Gaining the Rights of Citizenship

On April 9, 1865 the South surrendered. On April 15th Abraham Lincoln was assassinated. On April 20, Lincoln's Vice President, Democrat Andrew Johnson, formerly Governor of Tennessee, formally declared the war over.

The 11 Confederate states would reenter the Union. But left undecided was the legal status of ex-slaves. When slavery was abolished the Constitutional compromise that counted slaves as 3/5 of a person for purposes of Congressional representation no longer applied. After the 1870 Census the South's representation would be based on a full counting of 4 million ex-slaves. One Illinois Republican expressed a common fear that the "reward of treason will be an increased representation."

Between 1864 and 1866, ten of the eleven Confederate states inaugurated governments that did not provide suffrage and equal civil rights to freedmen. This was acceptable to Andrew Johnson but not to Republicans like Thaddeus Stevens, masterfully played in the movie by Tommy Lee Jones, who insisted that Reconstruction must "revolutionize Southern institutions, habits, and manners… The foundations of their institutions… must be broken up and relaid, or all our blood and treasure have been spent in vain."

In March 1865 Congress created the Freedmen's Bureau to provide food, clothing and fuel to ex-slaves and advice on negotiating labor contracts between freedmen and their former masters. The Bureau, not the local courts, handled the legal affairs of freedmen. It could lease confiscated land for a period of three years and sell portions of up to 40 acres per buyer.

When Johnson assumed the Presidency he ordered any confiscated or abandoned lands administered by the Freedman's Bureau returned to pardoned owners rather than redistributed to freedmen.

The Bureau was to expire one year after the termination of the War. In January 1866, Congress renewed the Act. Johnson vetoed the bill. An attempt to override the veto failed, marking the beginning of a struggle between Congress and the President over which branch of government had the ultimate authority to oversee Reconstruction—a struggle that ultimately led to the impeachment of Andrew Johnson by the House in 1868. He avoided removal from office by only one vote in the Senate.

In 1865 the Senate and House denied the seating of any Senator or Representative from the Confederate States until Congress decided when Reconstruction was finished.

In March 1866 Congress enacted the first Civil Rights bill, intended to give ex-slaves full legal equality. It stated, "All persons born in the United States … are hereby declared to be citizens of the United States; and such citizens of every race and color, without regard to any previous condition of slavery … shall have the same right in every State … to make and enforce contracts, to sue, be parties, and give evidence, to inherit, purchase, lease, sell, hold, and convey real and personal property, and to full and equal benefit of all laws and proceedings for the security of person and property, as is enjoyed by white citizens, and shall be subject to like punishment, pains, and penalties and to none other, any law, statute, ordinance, regulation, or custom to the Contrary notwithstanding."

Johnson vetoed the bill. This time Congress overrode his veto. (Congress also passed a more moderate Freedmen's Bureau Bill and overrode the subsequent Presidential veto of that.)

In response to the Civil Rights Act, every southern legislature passed "black codes," which limited the rights and civil liberties of freed slaves. Many stripped blacks of their right to vote, serve on juries, testify against whites and own firearms. Some declared that ex-slaves who failed to sign yearly labor contracts could be arrested and hired out to white landowners.

Congress then passed the Fourteenth Amendment, extending citizenship to everyone born in the United States and prohibiting anyone from being deprived of "life, liberty, or property, without due process of law" or denied "the equal protection of the laws." The Amendment also allowed federal courts to enforce these rights. The Southern states, with the exception of Tennessee and several border states, refused to ratify the Amendment.

A sweeping Republican victory in the 1866 Congressional elections gave Republicans a two-thirds majority, ushering in a ten-year period of aggressive efforts to defend the rights of ex-slaves. The 1867 Reconstruction Act required as a condition of readmittance to the Union for Southern states to ratify the 14th Amendment. The Act also placed the former Confederacy under military rule.

The army conducted new elections in which freed slaves could vote. Whites who had held leading positions under the Confederacy were not permitted to run for office. Republicans took control of all Southern state governorships and state legislatures, except Virginia.

The impact on Southern politics and culture was revolutionary. At the beginning of 1867, no African-American in the South held political office. Within three or four years about 15 percent of all elected officials in the South were black. It may be instructive to note that this was still far below blacks' proportion of the population, which was over 50 percent in Mississippi, Louisiana and South Carolina, and over 40 percent in four other Confederate states.

Biracial governments wrote new state constitutions, established public schools and charitable institutions and raised the extremely low taxes put in place largely because of the influence of plantation owners. Literacy rates rose dramatically.

In early 1870 Congress passed the 15th Amendment, which finally gave blacks, and other minorities, the right to vote.

Losing the Rights of Citizenship

By 1870 the legal structure was in place to provide ex-slaves full citizenship. The next decades put to the test Martin Luther King Jr's observation about the human condition expressed a century later. "(W)hile it may be true that morality cannot be legislated, behavior can be regulated. It may be true that the law cannot change the heart but it can restrain the heartless. It may be true that the law cannot make a man love me but it can keep him from lynching me…"

The South proved King wrong. A new civil war erupted, this time not between North and South but internal to the South. The Ku Klux Klan (KKK), the Red Shirts, the White League, the White Liners, and other paramilitary organizations operated openly and with clear political goals: the overthrow of Republican rule and the suppression of black voting. They became known as the "military arm of the Democratic Party."

In 1870 a wave of resulting assassinations in the South moved Congress to pass a law criminalizing conspiracies to deny black suffrage and empowering the President to use military troops to suppress organizations that deprived the rights guaranteed by the Fourteenth Amendment. Some 20,000 U.S. troops were deployed to enforce the law.

Largely as a result of this widespread violence and intimidation. Democrats had regained control of state legislatures in every southern state by 1877. At the federal level the Depression of 1873, the first major economic collapse in U.S. history and the Republicans' embrace of a fiscal policy that further contracted the economy led to the Democrat's controlling the House of Representatives in 1876 for the first time since 1856.

The tight 1876 Presidential election was thrown into the House of Representatives where Democrats agreed to support Rutherford Hayes, the Republican candidate, in return for his promise to completely withdraw federal troops from the South.

The federal courts proved unwilling to enforce the Constitution. In 1873 the Supreme Court ruled that the Fourteenth Amendment protected U.S. citizens from rights infringements only by the federal government, not states. In 1876, it ruled that only states, not the federal government, could prosecute individuals under the Ku Klux Klan Act. In 1883, it ruled that the Fourteenth Amendment applied only to discrimination from the government, not from individuals.

Having regained political control and no longer challenged by federal troops or federal courts the South began to systematically strip blacks of the vote, beginning with the Georgia poll tax in 1877. Later they began adding residency requirements, and literacy tests. States conveniently exempted any man whose father or grandfather had voted prior to January 1, 1867 from such requirements.

The impact on black suffrage was devastating. In 1896 in Louisiana, for example, where the population was evenly divided between races, 130,334 black voters were on the registration rolls, about the same number as whites. By 1900 the number of black registered voters had been reduced to 5,320 and by 1910 to only 730.

What came to be known as Jim Crow laws formalized the return of blacks to subordinate status, leading historian W.E.B. Du Bois to famously observe, "(T)he slave went free; stood a brief moment in the sun; then moved back again toward slavery."

This disenfranchisement of blacks attracted the attention of Congress. From 1896-1900, the House of Representatives set aside election results in over 30 cases where it concluded, "black voters had been excluded due to fraud, violence, or intimidation." But eventually these investigations died out as Democrats, repeatedly re-elected in one-party states, gained seniority in Congress, resulting in the control of important committees in both houses. Their Congressional power allowed them not only to end investigations into voter suppression but also to defeat anti-lynching legislation and other laws introduced to protect the rights of blacks.

Regaining Citizenship

In the 1940s, for the first time, the Supreme Court began enforcing the 14th and 15th amendments. In 1944 it outlawed all-white primaries. In 1946 it ruled that state laws requiring segregation on interstate buses were unconstitutional. In l950 it required Oklahoma to desegregate its schools. And in 1954 it declared all segregated schools inherently unequal.

The South proved intransigent, notwithstanding President Eisenhower sending federal troops into Little Rock to integrate Central High School in 1957, the first time federal troops were deployed in the South since 1877. Civil rights lawyer Michelle Alexander notes that ten years after the *Brown v. Board of Education* decision not a single black child attended an integrated grade school in South Carolina, Alabama or Mississippi. Five southern legislatures passed 50 new Jim Crow laws. White citizens councils formed in almost every town. The Ku Klux Klan reasserted itself.

But in the 1960s two new factors came into play. One was the advent of television which allowed the whole country to see Southern police using fire hoses and beating peacefully protesting blacks. The other was the rise of a large civil rights movement. "In the absence of a massive, grassroots movement directly challenging the racial caste system, Jim Crow might be alive and well today," Alexander writes. "Between autumn 1961 and spring 1963 20,000 men, women and children had been arrested [in civil rights protests]. In l963 alone, an additional l5,000 were imprisoned. One thousand desegregation protests occurred across the region in more than 100 cities."

In 1963 President John Kennedy announced he would introduce a civil rights bill. In January 1964 the Twenty Fourth

Amendment banned the use of poll taxes in federal elections. In July 1964 President Johnson signed the Civil Rights Act, which prohibited segregation in public places and barred unequal application of voter registration requirements.

In 1965 the Voting Rights Act passed. The Act outlawed literacy tests and provided for federal oversight. Section 5 required states and counties, inside and outside the South, with histories of voter discrimination against minorities to obtain approval from the Department of Justice before changing their voting laws.

The percentage of African American adults registered to vote soared. From 1964 to 1969 the rate in Alabama jumped from 19.3 to 61.3 percent, in Mississippi from 6.7 percent to 66.5 percent, in Georgia from 27.4 percent to 60.4 percent.

Nevertheless, 15 years after the passage of the Voting Rights Act only 8 percent of all Southern elected officials were black, about half the proportion that had held office a century earlier.

Mass Incarceration: The New Jim Crow

As barriers to voting and discrimination against social and economic discrimination fell one by one blacks, and increasingly Latinos, found themselves facing still another barrier to full citizenship: mass incarceration. In her book, *The New Jim Crow*, Alexander makes a persuasive case that the unprecedented growth in our prison population since the 1970s has been motivated by racial animus. John Erlichman, special counsel to Nixon has described Nixon's 1968 law-and-order Southern strategy as aimed at "the anti-black voter." Political scientist Vesla Weaver maintains, "Votes cast in opposition to open housing, busing, the Civil Rights Act and other measures time and again showed the same divisions as votes for amendments to crime bills…."

Ronald Reagan kicked off his Presidential campaign at the annual Neshoba county fair near Philadelphia, Mississippi the site of the 1964 murder of three civil rights activists, declaring, "I believe in states' rights."

In October 1982 Reagan kicked off a new war on drugs. At the time only 2 percent of the American public believed drugs were a major problem. Between 1981 and 1991 the Drug Enforcement Agency budget leaped from $86 million to $1 billion.

Until 1988 the maximum prison sentence for possession of any amount of any drug was one year. The 1988 Anti-Drug Abuse Act imposed dramatically longer mandatory sentences. In 1994 Bill Clinton upped the ante, sending a $30 billion crime bill to Congress and embracing a "one strike and you're out" policy in which authorities could evict any public housing tenant if a family member allows any form of drug related activity to occur in or near public housing. Congress imposed a lifetime ban on eligibility for welfare and food stamps for anyone convicted of a felony drug offense, even simple possession of marijuana. Students could become ineligible for loans if convicted of a drug offense.

From 1980 to 2000 the number of people in prisons or jails soared from 300,000 to more than 2 million.

Two thirds of the rise in the federal inmate population and more than half of the rise in state prisoners was for drug offenses. And as of 2005 as much as 80 percent of drug arrests were for possession.

Human Rights Watch reported in 2000 that in seven states African Americans constituted 80-90 percent of all drug offenders sent to prison. In at least 15 states blacks were admitted to prison on drug charges at a rate of 20-57 times greater than white men even though the majority of illegal drug users and dealers are white.

By the end of 2007 more than 7 million American were behind bars, on probation or parole. Less than two decades after war on drugs began 1 in 7 black men nationally have lost the right to vote and as many as one in four in some states. As legal scholar Pamela Karlan has observed, "felony disenfranchisement has decimated the potential black electorate."

The Supreme Court once again refused to enforce the Constitution by deciding in case after case that clear statistical evidence of racial bias in arrests or jury selection or judicial verdicts was not enough. The complainant had to prove intent.

Following the 2000 election, it was widely reported that had the 600,000 people convicted of felonies who had completed their sentences in Florida been allowed to vote Al Gore would have easily won the state and the presidency.

In 2008 a black man was elected President and re-elected in 2012. In 2012 more than 70 percent of Latinos and over 90 percent of blacks voted for Obama. Outside of the South he won about 45 percent of the white vote. But in the South he received, on average, only about 20 percent and only 10 percent in Mississippi and Alabama.

The Struggle Continues

Indeed, despite Obama's re-election and Democrats' gains in other states, the Republican control of the South tightened. For the first time since Reconstruction, Republicans took over the Arkansas legislature, and won the state's last U.S. House seat held by a Democrat. North Carolina elected a Republican governor and Republicans gained three more Congressional seats. The last Democrat in a statewide office in Alabama was defeated.

In most Southern states, the margins of victory for Mitt Romney were even larger than the lopsided margins for John McCain four years ago. *New York Times* reporter Campbell Robertson observed, "The racial and partisan divide is nearly absolute in the Deep South, with a Democratic Party that is almost entirely black and a Republican Party that is almost entirely white."

Within two weeks of the election the *Daily Caller* reported, "Petitions (for secession) from Alabama, Florida, Georgia, Louisiana, North Caroline, Tennessee and Texas residents have accrued at least 25,000 signatures, the number the Obama administration says it will reward with a staff review of online proposals." Texas Representative Ron Paul, Former Republican president candidate, lauded the petitions, declaring, "secession is a deeply American principle."

Meanwhile the Supreme Court has retreated from its aggressive defense of voting rights. In 1966 the Warren Court struck down a

$1.50 tax imposed on each voter (equivalent to about $10.50 today). Legislators in southern states defended the tax as a way to prevent "repeaters and floaters" from committing voter fraud. The Court ruled that voting is a fundamental Constitutional right and thus the burden was on the state to prove that a discriminatory law was necessary. It argued that a "payment of a fee as a measure of a voter's qualifications" violates the equal protection clause of the 14th Amendment by unfairly burdening low income, mostly black voters.

In 2007, in a case involving an extremely restrictive voter photo ID law in Indiana, the Roberts Court turned the Warren Court's 1966 decision on its head by deciding that the burden of proof now rests on those discriminated against to disprove "every conceivable basis which might support" the discrimination. Indiana offered no evidence to support the need for a photo ID. Indeed, it was unable to identify a single instance of in-person voter impersonation fraud in all of its history. The Court acknowledged that as many as 40,000 voters could be at risk because they would have to bear the cost of traveling to distant locations and paying up to $12 for a birth certificate or upwards of $100 for a passport to obtain such an ID, a far greater financial penalty than that imposed by the southern poll tax.

The Roberts Court decision unleashed a wave of voter restriction laws. Thirty states now have voter ID laws, many of them requiring a government-issued ID.

President Obama did win re-election, but the context of that victory is instructive. Elizabeth Drew writes in the *New York Review of Books*, "On election day, a nationwide coalition of lawyers manned five thousand call centers around the country. Its phone line 1-866-OUR-VOTE…was flooded with almost 100,000 calls from distressed voters saying that they had been told at the polling places that they weren't eligible to vote, even though they had registered." Some waited in line for 6 hours or more to exercise their right to vote.

In December 2011 the Department of Justice invoked the Voting Rights Act to block South Carolina's voter ID law. In August

2012 a three judge panel unanimously held that Florida could not slash its early voting period, citing the Voting Rights Act. After the election this year, the former chairman of the Florida Republican Party, in an interview with the Palm Beach Post noted that he went to several meetings in which Republican officials discussed the damage that early voting, which brought an unprecedented number of blacks to the polls in 2008, had done to the party.

In August another three-judge panel unanimously ruled that Texas' new state legislative and congressional districts diluted minority voting strength, citing the Voting Rights Act.

Three days after the 2012 election the Roberts Court announced it will hear Shelby County, Alabama's challenge to the Voting Rights Act. Most observers predict it will overturn the requirement that states gain Department of Justice (DOJ) approval for voting changes.

By all means go see the movie *Lincoln*. You can even go out cheering the January 1865 victory. But realize that the movie's triumphal ending did not mark the end of the struggle to gain full citizenship for blacks and other minorities, but only the beginning. Today minorities no longer confront poll taxes and the Ku Klux Klan but newly imposed voting restrictions and racially biased drug laws and a Supreme Court that is indifferent or outright hostile to the rights of minorities. Gridlocked Washington will not come to the rescue. But much of the problem lies at the state level. We need a new massive grassroots struggle such as that which arose in the 1950s and the 1960s, this one to overturn draconian and racially biased drug laws and to eliminate the new wave of law that hamper voter participation. The struggle continues.

America Is Beset by an Urban–Rural Divide

Brian Thiede, Steven Beda, Lillie Greiman, et al.

The authors are historians, sociologists, economists, and demographers at universities across the United States.

Editor's note: We've all heard of the great divide between life in rural and urban America. But what are the factors that contribute to these differences? We asked sociologists, economists, geographers, and historians to describe the divide from different angles. The data paint a richer and sometimes surprising picture of the U.S. today.

Poverty is higher in rural areas

Discussions of poverty in the United States often mistakenly focus on urban areas. While urban poverty is a unique challenge, rates of poverty have historically been higher in rural than urban areas. In fact, levels of rural poverty were often double those in urban areas throughout the 1950s and 1960s.

While these rural-urban gaps have diminished markedly, substantial differences persist. In 2015, 16.7 percent of the rural population was poor, compared with 13.0 percent of the urban population overall—and 10.8 percent among those living in suburban areas outside of principal cities.

Contrary to common assumptions, substantial shares of the poor are employed. Approximately 45 percent of poor, prime-age (25–54) householders worked at least part of 2015 in rural and urban areas alike.

The link between work and poverty was different in the past. In the early 1980s, the share of the rural poor that was employed exceeded that in urban areas by more than 15 percent. Since then,

American workers in poverty

Percent of US households aged 25-54 that worked at least part of the year
in 2015, by poverty threshold

■ <50% of poverty line

▨ 50-99% of poverty line

▨ 100-149% of poverty line

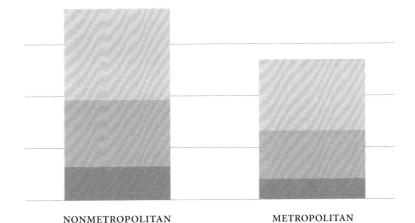

NONMETROPOLITAN   METROPOLITAN

SOURCE: 2016 March Current Publication Survey Public Use Microdata

more and more poor people in rural areas are also unemployed—a
trend consistent with other patterns documented below.

That said, rural workers continue to benefit less from work than
their urban counterparts. In 2015, 9.8 percent of rural, prime-age
working householders were poor, compared with 6.8 percent of
their urban counterparts. Nearly a third of the rural working poor
faced extreme levels of deprivation, with family incomes below
50 percent of the poverty line, or approximately US$12,000 for a
family of four.

Large shares of the rural workforce also live in economically
precarious circumstances just above the poverty line. Nearly one in
five rural working householders lived in families with incomes less

than 150 percent of the poverty line. That's nearly five percentage points more than among urban workers (13.5 percent).

According to recent research, rural-urban gaps in working poverty cannot be explained by rural workers' levels of education, industry of employment or other similar factors that might affect earnings. Rural poverty—at least among workers—cannot be fully explained by the characteristics of the rural population. That means reducing rural poverty will require attention to the structure of rural economies and communities.

– *Brian Thiede, Assistant Professor of Rural Sociology and Demography, Pennsylvania State University*

Most new jobs aren't in rural areas

It's easy to see why many rural Americans believe the recession never ended: For them, it hasn't.

Job growth in America

Since 2018, job growth in metropolitan areas has outpaced that in rural areas.

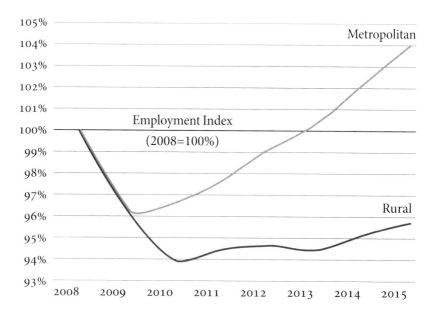

SOURCE: Integrated Public Use Microdata Series: Version 6.0, 2008-2015 ACS

Rural communities still haven't recovered the jobs they lost in the recession. Census data show that the rural job market is smaller now—4.26 percent smaller, to be exact—than it was in 2008. In these data are shuttered coal mines on the edges of rural towns and boarded-up gas stations on rural main streets. In these data are the angers, fears and frustrations of much of rural America.

This isn't a new trend. Mechanization, environmental regulations and increased global competition have been slowly whittling away at resource extraction economies and driving jobs from rural communities for most of the 20th century. But the fact that what they're experiencing now is simply the cold consequences of history likely brings little comfort to rural people. If anything, it only adds to their fear that what they once had is gone and it's never coming back.

Nor is it likely that the slight increase in rural jobs since 2013 brings much comfort. As the resource extraction economy continues to shrink, most of the new jobs in rural areas are being created in the service sector. So Appalachian coal miners and Northwest loggers are now stocking shelves at the local Walmart.

The identity of rural communities used to be rooted in work. The signs at the entrances of their towns welcomed visitors to coal country or timber country. Towns named their high school mascots after the work that sustained them, like the Jordan Beetpickers in Utah or the Camas Papermakers in Washington. It used to be that, when someone first arrived at these towns, they knew what people did and that they were proud to do it.

That's not so clear anymore. How do you communicate your communal identity when the work once at the center of that identity is gone, and calling the local high school football team the "Walmart Greeters" simply doesn't have the same ring to it?

Looking at rural jobs data, is it so hard to understand why many rural people are nostalgic for the past and fearful for the future?

– *Steven Beda, Instructor of History, University of Oregon*

Disabilities are more common in rural areas

Disability matters in rural America. Data from the American Community Survey, an annual government poll, reveal that disability is more prevalent in rural counties than their urban counterparts.

The rate of disability increases from 11.8 percent in the most urban metropolitan counties to 15.6 percent in smaller micropolitan areas and 17.7 percent in the most rural, or noncore, counties.

Disability Rates

Rates of disability increase from more urban (metropolitan) to more rural (non-core) counties.

Metropolitan: counties with an urban population of 50,000+   11.8

Micropolitan: counties with an urban population of 10,000-50,000   15.6

Non-core: counties with an urban population of less than 10,000   17.7

SOURCE: RTC: Rural

While rural-urban differences in disability have been analyzed previously, researchers have had little opportunity to further explore this disparity, as updated data on rural disability were unavailable until recently. Fortunately, the census released updated new county-level disability estimates in 2014, ending a 14-year knowledge gap.

The release of these estimates has also allowed us to build a picture of geographic variations in disability across the nation. Disability rates vary significantly across the U.S. Although the national trend of higher disability rates in rural counties persists at the regional and even divisional level, it is clear that disability in rural America is not homogeneous. Rates of rural disability range from around 15 percent in the Great Plains to 21 percent in the central South.

A variety of factors may be behind these regional and rural differences, including differences in demographics, economic patterns, health and service access and state disability policies.

While this survey provides a glimpse into the national prevalence of disability and reveals a persistent rural-urban disparity, it is important to note its limitations. Disability is the result of an interaction between an individual and his or her environment. Therefore, these data do not directly measure disability, as they measure only physical function and do not consider environmental factors such as inaccessible housing.

– Lillie Greiman and Andrew Myers, Project Directors at the Rural Institute for Inclusive Communities at the University of Montana; Christiane von Reichert, Professor of Geography, University of Montana

Rural areas are surprisingly entrepreneurial

The United States' continuing economic dominance is perhaps most attributable to the very smallest elements of its economy: its entrepreneurial start-ups. Nearly 700,000 new job-creating businesses open each year. That's almost 2,000 every day, each helping to create new market niches in the global economy.

Most people mistakenly believe these pioneering establishments occur in overwhelmingly in metropolitan areas, such as in the now-mythic start-up culture of Silicon Valley.

Yet, according to the U.S. Census Bureau, it is in fact nonmetropolitan counties that have higher rates of self-employed business proprietors than their metropolitan counterparts.

Furthermore, the more rural the county, the higher its level of entrepreneurship. Some of these counties have a farming legacy— perhaps the most entrepreneurial of occupations—but farmers represent less than one-sixth of business owners in nonmetro areas. Even for nonfarm enterprises, rural entrepreneurship rates are higher.

The reality is that rural areas have to be entrepreneurial, as industries with concentrations of wage and salary jobs are necessarily scarce.

Start-up businesses have notoriously difficult survival prospects. So it is perhaps even more surprising that relatively isolated nonmetropolitan businesses are on average more resilient than their metro cousins, despite the considerable economic advantages of urban areas, which boast a denser networks of workers, suppliers and markets. The resilience of rural start-ups is perhaps due to more cautious business practices in areas with few alternative employment options.

This resilience is also remarkably persistent over time, consistently being at least on par with metro start-ups, and regularly having survival rates up to 10 percentage points higher than in metro areas over 1990-2007.

– Stephan Weiler, Professor of Economics, Colorado State University; Tessa Conroy and Steve Deller, Professors of Economics, University of Wisconsin-Madison

The Urban-Rural Divide Isn't Just Geographical, It's Ideological

Raza Rumi

Raza Rumi is scholar in residence in the Department of Journalism at Ithaca College. His writing has appeared in Foreign Affairs, *the* Huffington Post, *and the* New York Times, *among other outlets.*

S ince the historic win of Donald Trump, the American media and pundits have been grappling to understand the election results and their inability to predict the turn of events. It will take some time before detailed data on actual voter behavior is made available but one trend is clear. Voters who live in large urban centers largely voted for Hillary Clinton while those who live in more rural parts of the country voted for Donald Trump.

The ideological divide manifested itself through the vast geography of the United States. The reasons are linked to the inequities that define today's America and how its citizenry is divided along class lines. The residents of cities are typically wealthier, have higher educational attainment and are somewhat more liberally inclined. Conversely, many rural parts of the U.S. are poorer and are less educated in the formal sense.

These generalizations admittedly are challenged by many exceptions but the electoral maps attest that the blue (Democratic) clusters are in cities and the Republican support is strongest in the vast lands of rural America.

Most states where one party controls both branches of the legislature (State House & Senate) are gerrymandered in the ruling parties favor. The 2016 presidential election county-by-county map shows that the urban rural divide has been further intensified by gerrymandering. When districts are drawn to shepherd Democrats and Republicans into their own corners

"2016 Election Explainer In 4 Words: The Urban-Rural Divide," by Raza Rumi, TheHuffingtonPost.com, Inc., December 9, 2016. Reprinted by Permission.

(in different parts of a state), this makes the disparities in their voting patterns even more vibrant and obvious on an electoral map. Instead of a balance of conservatives and liberals, a mix of red and blue spread out across a state, gerrymandering essentially segregates and silos D's and R's into their own subsections as you'll see below.

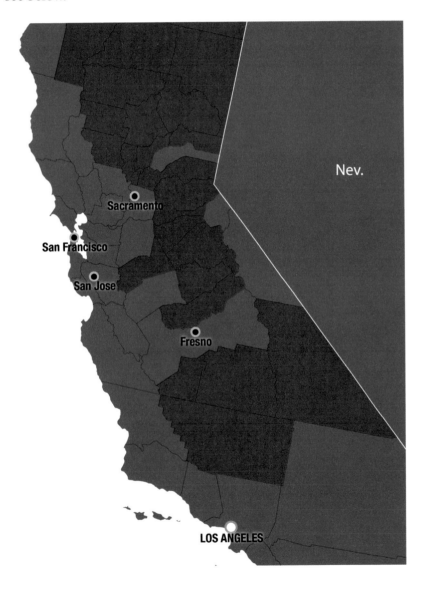

Red Rubies on the Democratic West Coast

Blue Urban Pockets: San Francisco, LA, Sacramento, Seattle, Portland
*Red Rolling Rural-lands: Most of Oregon, Washington and half
of California*

All along the "lefty liberal" designated Democrat west coast, there
were large swathes of red. Half of California, the supposed holy grail
of the Democratic party west of the Mississippi, voted for Trump.

The counties that went blue were invariably clustered around
the urban centers of Sacramento, San Francisco, LA and San
Diego. Further up in Oregon and Washington, the blue zones
were not surprisingly concentrated around the large metropolises
of Portland and Seattle respectfully.

Outside of the city centers, the rural populace of two
northwest states—Oregon and Washington—voted for Trump.
Most rural areas all along the west coast voted Republican. On
the map, these appear as red Trumpian rubies, in an otherwise
blue jewelry shop.

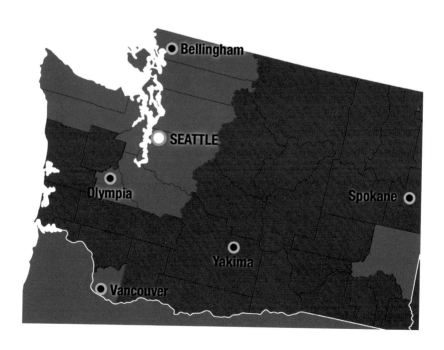

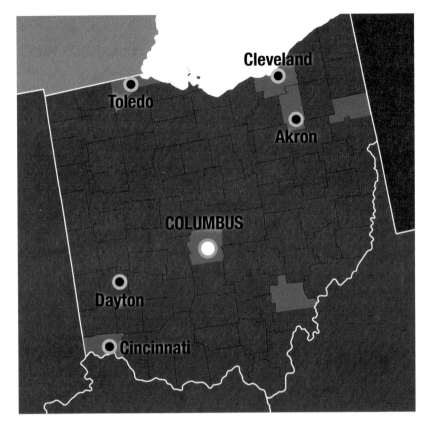

The [Wild] Mid West

Tiny Blue Urban Pockets: Chicago, Cleveland, Madison, Milwaukee, Cincinnati, Columbus

Red Rolling Rural-lands: Everywhere else where people live farther apart

Ohio has always been a deal breaker as the perennial swing state. The results from the recent election show how the state is marked by blue polka dots on an otherwise red dress.

These dots are its urban centers of Cleveland, Akron, Columbus and Cincinnati. Although the state went to Trump, the cities went to Clinton.

The same occurred in Clinton's original home state of Illinois, where the counties around the Midwestern capital, Chicago, went blue whereas most of the rest of the state went red. Overall the state

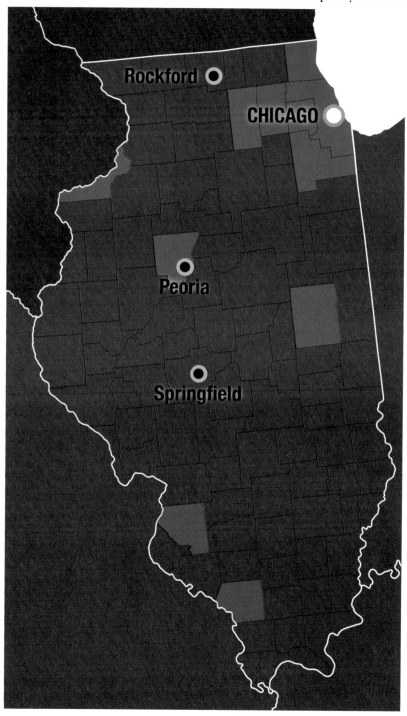

went to the Democrats because of the high density of people that live in the Chicago metropolitan area and Peoria, these two cities had more people within them that voted for Clinton than practically the rest of the entire state's counties which voted for Trump.

Lastly, in Wisconsin that has historically been a blue stronghold (Clinton hasn't visited the State once since the Democratic convention because it was considered a safe win), surprisingly went to Trump. This happened because unlike in Illinois, the urban centers of Madison, Milwaukee and Eau Claire didn't have enough Democrats voting for Clinton to tilt the overall outcome. The rest of the (mostly) rural state, went to Trump.

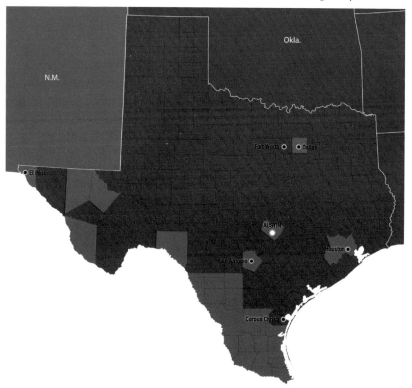

The South Is Not Another Country

*Tiny Blue Urban Pockets: Austin, Dallas, San Antonio, Houston,
New Orleans, Baton Rouge*
*Red Rolling Rural-lands: Everywhere else where millions of people
are not congregated*

Even in the deeply red republic of Texas, the large economic,
political and cultural capitals of Austin, Dallas, Houston and San
Antonio voted for Clinton. Republicans control all statewide Texas
offices and both houses of the state legislature.

Texas has voted Republican in in every presidential election
since 1980. Despite this history, its urban centers are perennially
blue, along with a number of counties situated on the border,
where Democratic leaning Hispanics make up a larger proportion
of the population.

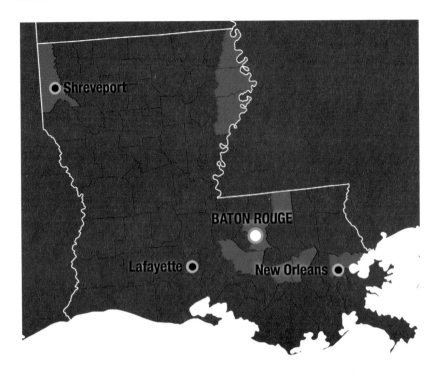

In Louisiana too, the large metropolis of New Orleans along with its second largest city, Baton Rouge went blue while the rest of the historically Republican state remained true to its past. Like Texas, the cities were not dominant enough to swing the state for Clinton.

The rural vote enabled Trump to win both state.

East Is East

Tiny Blue Urban Pockets: NYC, Syracuse, Rochester, Buffalo, Miami, Orlando, Tampa, Richmond, Alexandria
Red Rolling Rural-lands: Everywhere else where tall concrete structures don't exist

New York has been a Democratic stronghold for years now. It is also Clinton's current home state. Yet, if it weren't for New York City's millions of voters, the state might have gone Trump red. Other than the urban centers of Syracuse, Buffalo, Rochester and Albany, almost all of upstate New York voted for Trump.

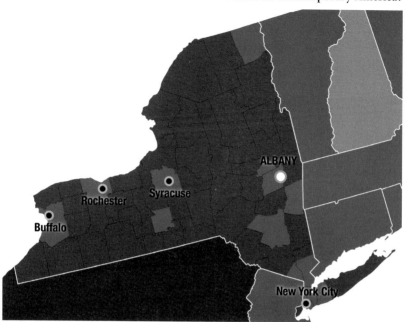

Virginia displayed the same pattern where the urban zones of
Alexandria (right next to D.C.), Richmond and Norfolk, tipped
a mostly red state into Clinton territory. The urban-rural, blue-
red divide is particularly evident here with Roanoke, which looks
like a blue coliseum, surrounded by red soldiers. Part of this is
also due to the electoral district gerrymandering, which has taken
place in the past.

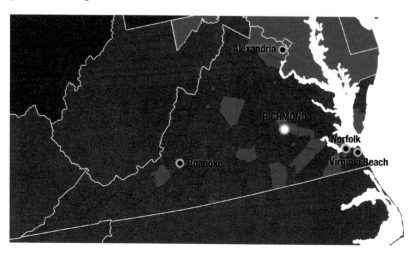

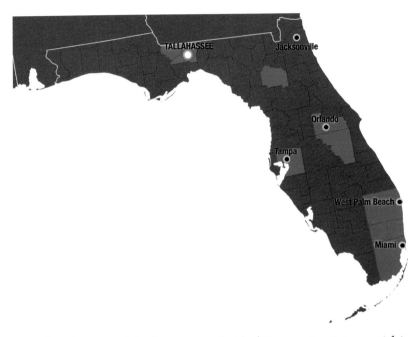

Florida, one of the key states that led Trump to victory within the Electoral College, confirmed the same divide. Cities—Miami, Orlando, Tampa and Tallahassee—voted for Clinton while the rest of the rural landscape was painted red by Trump's rhetoric.

Pundits are now asking Trump to unite the country. While semantics are important the real unity in the U.S. requires thinking long and hard about the economic and political forces that deindustrialized and depressed large swaths of rural America.

The impoverished, the less advantaged and the marginalized America spoke on Nov. 8th.

The Supposed Urban-Rural Divide Is a False Dichotomy

Courtney Martin

Courtney Martin is an essayist and cultural critic. Her latest book, The New Better Off: Reinventing the American Dream, *reorients the famous aspiration toward fulfillment and community.*

Carol Coletta, the president and CEO of Chicago-based CEOs for Cities, directed the 100 or so young, urban leaders seated before her to look up at a map of the United States as she demonstrated the steady migration of Americans out of rural areas and into cities over the last 10 years. Little blue dots representing the population piled inward and on top of one another like bees to a honeyed hive. Coletta is a true city evangelist, as were most of those in attendance at last week's Urban Next Summit conference in San Francisco.

There's no question that cities are where the action and attention are largely focused these days. According to the U.S. government, 80 percent of Americans live in an urban setting. One of President Barack Obama's first orders of office was to create a White House Office of Urban Affairs, not a surprising move for a man who won the election with city dwellers by a margin of 28 points. Richard Florida's 2003 bestseller, *Rise of the Creative Class*, argued that technology, talent, and tolerance were the three keys to attracting the next generation of wealth producers/consumers to a city.

It's all pretty convincing—in this tough domestic economy, with increasing competition abroad, it is the health and wealth of our cities that will determine our collective future.

But before we write the obituary for the American outback, it behooves us to look at a contemporary twist on the urbanist tale. There's a new "creative class" in town. Or, more accurately, out of town. Increasingly, young entrepreneurs, activists, and small-business owners are trying to make lives that blend the wildness of the city with the wellness of the country.

Last week, you could have easily found Jerri Chou, 27, pecking away at her Mac laptop, headphones on, eyes intermittently pulled up from her screen by the striking beauty of the Brooklyn Bridge just outside her DUMBO office window. She was planning a conference on social entrepreneurship, in between attending U.N. meetings, and blogging for the organization that she co-founded, Alldaybuffet.com, a virtual think tank of sorts for cutting-edge do-gooders.

But this woman-about-town isn't satisfied with an exclusively urban existence. Starting in 2009, she began working on a collaborative farm and retreat center called Ananda Ashram located in Harriman, New York. She and a group of about 10 other young New Yorkers spend as little as a weekend and as much as a month at a time digging trenches, weeding and tending plants, splitting shingles, learning about permaculture, and just plain unplugging and laying near the lake.

"I'm drawn to it because I find there is so much to be learned about the world and ourselves from experiencing nature," Chou explains. "I'm sensitive to patterns, timing, and systems. Much of my work has to do with systems thinking, and there's no better example of that than the systems that nature has created."

On the other side of the country, 25-year-old Cole Bush spends about two weeks a month in the Bay Area, where she designs and maintains low-irrigation gardens for private clients, and the rest of her time in the coastal hills of Santa Cruz, where she lives and works part-time on a collective homestead called Trout Gulch with 14 other people (about half of them friends under the age of 35 who met in San Francisco).

Bush, who says she's attempting to "have her cake and eat it too," sees herself as part of a new wave of young people rejecting their suburban upbringings (she grew up North County San Diego), in favor of a hybrid rural-urban life.

"I exist in two worlds," she explains. "One is embedded in a
vibrant, yet peaceful setting, where I interact with the processes of
nature daily; one brings another quality of life, where the density
of resources allows me to travel on foot, bike, or public transit to
have rich cultural and creative experiences."

Of course Chou and Bush still constitute a minority; it's not easy
to compose such a flexible life and still sustain oneself economically.
Most of the young people who are making it work seem to get by
on very little money, depending on the kindness of friends who let
them couch surf or camp out (depending on where their primary
residence is), and avoiding some of the more typical big expenses
of the 20-something urban lifestyle (bar tabs, trendy clothes, new
gadgets). Their desire to combine the opportunities afforded by
urban life with the tranquility abundant in rural life can also be
seen in a variety of explosive trends that require less investment
and flexibility: rooftop gardens and farmers markets, the local-food
movement, and WOOF exchanges, whereby people basically do
work study on organic farms, waking up in the wee hours of the
day to offer their labor in exchange for a place to stay, fresh food
to eat, and an opportunity to learn about farming.

Placestory blogger, 31-year-old Molly May, says, "I'm done
with polarizing urban and rural. One sets off the other. Both
are vibrant."

She and her husband recently moved from an apartment in
Manhattan—filled with herbs they harvested from Central Park—
to a yurt in Montana—complete with solar power for their laptops.

Even city evangelists like Coletta recognize that the future of
cities depends, in part, on their capacity to incorporate some of
the best qualities of rural spaces into planning efforts. As part of
CEOs for Cities' U.S. initiative, they are inviting people to imagine
a new American Dream that has five ambitions, including: "We
will all have access to beauty and nature every day."

The era of juxtaposed city slickers and country bumpkins is
eroding, and in its place, the possibility to be both wired and
well, networked and natural, is taking shape. The great Wendell

Berry wrote, "You can best serve civilization by being against what usually passes for it." We have long accepted that we must choose between the excitement of the city or the beauty of the country, but as Berry urges, we are beginning to reject the deadening dichotomy altogether.

The Urban-Rural Divide Obscures the Ambitions that Unite All Americans

David Korten

David Korten cofounded Yes Magazine, *a publication devoted to political analysis and fostering civic engagement.*

Much has been made of the split between urban voters who favored Democrats and rural voters who favored Republicans. Trump prevailed by speaking directly to the pain of the voters who felt the most deeply betrayed by a system that once offered them jobs with attractive wages, security, and generous benefits. The jobs themselves, however, were often dangerous, dirty, and exhausting—coal mining being an extreme example. Others were mind-numbingly monotonous.

Those who endured the downside of these jobs took pride in their ability to support their families in comfort and dignity without need for government handouts. They valued their contributions to their communities and to America's position in the world.

Most of those well-compensated, unionized, working-class jobs have disappeared. Those who once held them—or aspired to hold them—are understandably angry. They want back the jobs, dignity, and sense of service an unjust system now denies them.

Despite Trump's glib promise and the hopes of those who trusted him more than they trusted Hillary Clinton, those jobs are not coming back. The impact of the trade agreements that facilitated the initial outsourcing of those jobs is now superseded by the impact of automation. Moving robots from China to the United States will not bring back the jobs that automation is rapidly eliminating. We must adapt our economic institutions to these realities to meet the needs of all—including our need for

"No Rural-Urban Divide Here: We All Want Good Jobs and Strong Local Economies," by David Korten, Yes Magazine, April 5, 2017. http://www.yesmagazine.org/new-economy/no-rural-urban-divide-here-we-all-want-good-jobs-and-strong-local-economies-20170405. Licensed Under CC BY-NC-ND 4.0 International.

dignity and self-respect—in ways consistent with the limits of a finite planet.

Local control is a foundational conservative principle. Many progressives embrace that principle as well, with a call to seek solutions in local economies grounded in local ownership. This area of agreement provides a potential foundation for an effective rural-urban political alliance to establish control of jobs, resources, markets, and finance in the hands of people who have a stake in the long-term economic, environmental, and social health of the communities in which they live.

A corporation that exhausts the soils, fisheries, or forests of one place simply moves to another, leaving the people to bear the consequences. This is an essential difference between people and corporations. People have a natural interest in prioritizing long-term health and well-being over short-term profits.

It is no coincidence that many of the worst pockets of poverty are located next to profitable, polluting, highly mechanized and automated resource extraction and processing sites—think fracking, mountaintop removal, tar sands, oil refineries, and chemical plants that destroy essential life-supporting resources, including clean water, fertile soils, healthy forests, and fisheries on which both rural and urban people ultimately depend. The profits go to corporations. Local communities live with the loss. Other pockets of poverty are located next to the world's remaining fertile lands and productive forests and fisheries—from which local people are excluded by the distant corporations that control and profit from them.

What if we cut out the corporate middlemen and restored control to the people who now bear the costs? The natural incentives would shift from favoring dirty fossil fuel energy to favoring local generation of clean wind and solar energy serving both rural and nearby urban consumers.

Instead of favoring mechanized, chemical-dependent agriculture that destroys soil, water, and jobs, natural incentives would favor labor-intensive organic agriculture that provides rural and urban consumers with healthy fresh food while restoring soil, sequestering carbon, replenishing aquifers, and significantly reducing dependence on chemical fertilizers and pesticides produced by automated, polluting, mining-dependent factories.

Forests and fisheries can be managed for healthy sustainable yields by the people who live next to them. And small scale factories using 3D printing and locally recycled materials can employ former industrial workers to meet many of our manufacturing needs.

The political divide in the United States need not be so wide as it currently seems. With a common vision of what we really want, we can work together to restructure economies to put control where it belongs—in the hands of local people who care for the health of themselves, the land on which they live, and the future of their children.

CHAPTER 2

Does Popular Culture Have the Power to Unite the Country?

Overview: Culture Friction and Conflicts Then and Now

Jon Kofas

Jon Kofas is an Indiana University professor emeritus in social sciences and a novelist.

Based on the bourgeois ideals and value system of the Enlightenment, Western open societies are culturally pluralistic but have limits in social cohesion owing to the hierarchical structure created by the political economy of capitalism. Symptomatic of the market economy, social differentiation and exclusion are a permanent fixture regardless of what the social contract promises about social integration. Founded as a colony of immigrants who conquered the lands of North America and used Africans as slave labor, America carries the legacy of contradictions from the Age of the Enlightenment promising egalitarianism and integration but in practice institutionalizing social exclusion and differentiation that precludes social cohesion. These contradictions become intense in periods of economic expansion or contraction when fissures are exposed on the surface of the social structure because socially excluded groups strive to integrate into the mainstream and demand its reform. Such societal fissures undermining social cohesion are more evident in American society in the second decade of the 21st century than they have been since the 1960s.

According to post-presidential election polls in 2016, America is more divided than at any time in post-WWII era, a reality that filters down from the political, corporate media and financial elites to ordinary people as skeptical about the legitimacy of their institutions as the elites. Republicans supporting the populist rightwing President Donald Trump have revived "Clash of Civilizations" (Samuel Huntington's work, 1996) as a core value

"Divided America: Root Causes and the Road Ahead?" by Jon Kofas, Counter Currents. org, January 17, 2017. Reprinted by Permission.

in US foreign policy in order to distract from the widening social divisions and presumably forge greater unification under a common foreign enemy. This theory as Republicans interpret it has broad ramifications for immigration policy, race and ethnic/religious relations and issues related to multiculturalism in an open society whose financial elites view the population as the consuming public than citizen with constitutional rights.

The US is a divided society amidst its own socioeconomic and political polarization reflected in clash of cultures shaped in part by a changing demography and shrinking middle class. While Trump Republicans are looking to "Clash of Civilization" as a means of projecting strength and rallying popular support for the flag, their Democrat opponents are trying their best to revive the Cold War US-Russian confrontation as a catalyst to appeasing the militarist and corporate elites while unifying their divided popular base. Both strategies are manifestations of a bankrupt political system that perpetuates divisions and foments more domestic culture clashes and is dumbfounded about how to deal with the contradictions of social exclusion and differentiation that has become intensified under neoliberal policies in a climate of globalization.

If people link their identity to culture and religion, according to those espousing the "Clash of Civilization" theory intended to explain the post-Cold root causes of future global conflict, then logic dictates that the same holds true for people of different cultures, religions, ethnicities, races, and ideologies inside the US. Considering the multicultural nature of the US demographic map and the dominant culture and institutions under the control of the descendants of European immigrants, culture clashes are just as inevitable when the country fails to deliver what people perceive as the social contract, namely the American Dream and keeping the nation strong in relationship to the rest of the world as Manifest Destiny promised when European immigrants created God's "New Israel" in North America.

To maintain political consensus among the disparate political, military, economic and socio-cultural elites "Clash of Civilizations" makes as much sense for Trump Republicans as the anti-Russia campaign does for Democrats. This is especially so in light of a Trump return to a Reagan-style "rightwing revolution," particularly with regard to fiscal policy as the Republicans will be transferring even more wealth from the bottom 90% of the population to the top 10% by trimming social programs and raising the cost of government by contracting out more public services at a higher cost and less efficiency than if government kept control.

While trying to expand their popular base, Republicans and the conservative media promote culture clashes as a means of mobilizing popular support among largely religious and cultural conservatives. This is especially in the white community that feels besieged in the age of globalization which has entailed de-industrialization and downward wage pressure; a phenomenon that has resulted in greater social exclusion from a group that identifies itself as representative of national values. Democrats and their supporters in the media also promote division largely by remaining focused on identity politics rather than restoring America's eroding middle class and working class living standards. Culture clashes manifest themselves in congress and state legislatures over all sorts of issues, some with very broad significance such as health care others linked to narrow identity politics and lifestyle issues; all indicative of social exclusion from an institutional mainstream that claims its foundation are rooted in inclusion.

There are cultural, ideological, political divisions so deep among disparate groups that one encounters two very different Americas when traveling from San Francisco, California to Jackson, Mississippi. The concept of America as an open society may very well apply to major cities, especially coastal and urban upper Midwest, but it is a stretch for much of the rest of the country. The media, political and institutional endeavors to suppress class consciousness and opt for identity politics and culture clashes only points to cracks in solidarity among the working class and middle class against the elites lining up behind the two major parties. Because social exclusion and differentiation assumes different socio-cultural forms in different parts of the country, the political elites are able to divide the population against itself and undermine class solidarity of socially excluded groups.

Public opinion polls in 2012 indicated that 69% of Americans viewed their nations divided, while that number jumped to 77%-80% right after the November general election in 2016. Just as significant, they indicate dissatisfaction with the way their society functions and see their prospects becoming worse not better. These same people do not see the forging of consensus any time soon, and fully expect deeper divisions, thus reflecting recognition of social exclusion and differentiation. A reflection of deep divisions, public opinion polls a few days before inauguration range from 37% to 44% approval rating for Trump, a historic low since such polls were conducted in 1992. As disturbing as such low numbers may be given that they are below those of the outgoing president's, an even greater concern is that they will only decline going forward once congress implements policies resulting in lower integration and greater exclusion.

This does not mean that non-urban, southern and Plains States America is any more racist, xenophobic, Islamophobic, sexist and less tolerant of non-natives than their counterparts in Russia, France, or Germany where there is a rise of ultra-rightwing political movements not much different than the populist wing of the Republican Party. Social exclusion and differentiation exists in all capitalist societies, some like the Scandinavian less, others, like Russia more. The demographic structure of US is changing and the realization of that incontrovertible fact has many whites reacting with anger amid eroding living standards and the economic pie so unevenly divided.

Naturally, an apologist of the status quo could argue that the US is hardly the world's most divided nation, considering there are developing nations immersed in civil wars or under authoritarian regimes that maintain the status quo by police methods. Apologists of the status quo point to developing nations as authoritarian and to the US remaining a defender of human rights and civil rights, despite a record of government practices that indicate otherwise. Apologists of the status quo refuse to accept that developed Western nations are experiencing the rise of extreme rightwing political parties challenging the neoliberal centrist and conservative ruling elites. This "revolution" from the extreme right will result in even deeper divisions across the entire Western World as societies claiming the legacy of 18th century Enlightenment ideals of John Locke's liberalism and Jean-Jacques Rousseau's social democracy are evolving from liberal capitalism to an authoritarian neoliberal capitalist model. (Ian Bruff, "The Rise of Authoritarian Neoliberalism", Rethinking Marxism, Vol. 26, Issue 1, 2014)

American Divisions in Historical Perspective

American colonists and immigrants were bound by the common goal to seek a better material life and enjoy freedom from religious persecution. However, these freedoms never translated equally for all ethnic groups and social classes in a country founded as a colony of the British Empire to advance its imperial economic and geopolitical interests. Indicative of the lack of social cohesion and political consensus among the colonists, when the War of Independence was declared, Americans were hardly as united behind the independence movement. Interested in national self-determination, largely wealthy white colonists led the revolution at a time that the colonies had slavery as an entrenched institution. Representing the landowning and commercial class, the Founding Fathers drafted a constitution declaring all men are created equal but in practice social differentiation and exclusion prevailed.

The chasm between what is declared in the Constitution about equality, freedom, and the pursuit of happiness and the reality in practice is at the heart of America's historical divisions. The famous July 1852 speech "What, to the Slave, is the Fourth of July?" by Frederick Douglas reveals the deep divisions in American society that has relevance to this day. "The existence of slavery in this country brands your republicanism as a sham, your humanity as a base pretence, and your Christianity as a lie. It destroys your moral power abroad; it corrupts your politicians at home. … it breeds insolence; it promotes vice; it shelters crime; it is a curse to the earth that supports it; and yet, you cling to it, as if it were the sheet anchor of all your hopes."

Historical divisions and culture clashes stem from the gap between the political principles of equality and justice for all, and the reality of wealthy predominantly Anglo-Saxon protestant elites that owned most of the wealth and enjoyed institutional privileges from education to elected office. Institutional obstacles to progress for the lower classes, women, and minorities were overcome throughout the Republic's history by peoples' attraction to the promise of the constitution about equality and the pursuit of happiness for all, and by the prospect of integration into the institutional mainstream where the elites enjoyed society's privileges. As long as the economy expanded and the social structure evolved to permit working people to move into the lower middle class and their children to secure education and create a better life, people conformed to the hegemonic culture and subordinated socio-cultural differences to the system that rewarded them at least in the domain of religious freedom and the promise for a better life.

Despite massive economic expansion as a result of the Westward expansion, industrialization, and imperialist expansion in the form of the Spanish-American War (1898), society remained at war with itself through the struggles of workers to unionize, women and immigrants to achieve equality of opportunity as their Western European white male counterparts, and blacks fighting to end institutionalized racism that is a permanent feature of America at war with itself.

Unlike ethnically and culturally homogenous societies, America as a nation of immigrants that conquered the natives is at war with itself because its only common value system is the immigrant dream of wealth and cultural freedom. Deeply imbedded in the consciousness of the people are Manifest Destiny and the dream of greatness, even if by association.

It is not only the case that 71% of Americans are Christians, but that there is a longstanding tradition of linking politics to Christian doctrine (America as God's country with a mandate from Divine Providence). This has been the case from its early history to the present and it has been an integral part of the social contract that the elites have used to forge consensus and conformity among the masses. (Nicole Guetin, *Religious Ideology and American Politics*, 2009) Although the same phenomenon is less evident in urban-suburban areas and Coastal and upper Mid-Western areas where secularism and a more cosmopolitan culture prevail, the concept of expansion and America's greatness mandated by divine providence is an unspoken underlying assumption. The degree to which political and financial elites can rely on religious leaders to help engender sociopolitical conformity and mitigate systemic divisions is an open question, although Christendom has been the catalyst to sociopolitical conformity for many centuries.

The merging of pseudo-science and religion, Social Darwinism and creationism in American history has helped to maintain sociopolitical conformity to the institutional mainstream from the 19th century to the present. As a nation that took the concept of competition more seriously than Adam Smith, Americans found it easy to merge Social Darwinism that assumed human progress rested on competition which is found in nature. It is indeed remarkable that no less than twenty-four states enacted 'sterilization eugenics legislation' between 1911 and 1930 intended to "weed out" the mentally ill and criminals, and the American Eugenics Society advocated laws to limit inter-racial marriages.

While Social Darwinism was popular among certain segments of society rejecting the concept of social cohesion and integration for all people as the US Constitution promises, creationism reinforced social exclusion and differentiation. With deep historical roots in culture clashes, creationist beliefs remain prominent just below the surface with a substantial percentage of Americans. In 2014, 42% of Americans believed in the creationist view of human origins, down 2% from 1982 when Reagan and the Moral Majority were contributing to the culture clash against those they demonized as humanist liberals. According to various public opinion polls, 13-28% of Americans responded that God was not involved in the creation of human beings and that evolution was responsible for life as we know it, while 51% accept the Bible as the word of God. By contrast, 69% of Britons believe in Darwin's theory of evolution, and 61% of Canadians. The striking differences are a manifestation of far greater social cohesion in the neighboring nation to the north also a former colony with not such a strikingly different historical experience.

A society steeped in the psychology of realizing its potential of greatness as Divine Providence mandated necessarily finds itself at odds its own disparate elites vying for influence and control to determine the nation's destiny and preserve their privileges, while socially excluded groups struggle for integration. Advocates of the Enlightenment secular ideology as the foundation of modern society clashing with the more conservative ad religious-oriented groups associating secularism with the privileged elites have been a permanent fixture in society. Clashes become more evident in times of glaring contradictions of economic expansion but contracting living standards. While social cohesion and integration is important to the political and financial elites in order to maintain stability in the political economy and social order, the same system produced greater social exclusion and differentiation.

De-legitimizing of the Political System

In a fierce power struggle, the Democrat Party and Republican Party elites have been delegitimizing each other in the eyes of the public. Political de-legitimization was evident ever since Barack Obama became the first black president. Although many conservatives viewed Obama's election as the end of white political monopoly of the executive branch of government, there was hardly any change in social integration and social exclusion under an administration that faithfully served the same elites as all its predecessors. In the 2016 primary season, Trump accused his Republican opponents and Democrat nominee Hillary Clinton of serving Wall Street for a price. Trump de-legitimized all others except himself because they were conduits of social exclusion. During the presidential election season, the increased journalistic interest regarding the division of American society assumed added dimensions largely because of the surprised election of Trump, now enjoying a Republican majority in the Senate and House of Representatives, as well as in most state governments and in the judicial branch.

Skepticism about legitimacy continued when the Democrats did everything they could to link Trump's election to alleged Russian hacking, one of the major distraction issues regardless of whether Russians were involved or not. This does not even take into account social media "fake news" and mainstream media intense propaganda campaigns reflecting and promoting the culture clash among disparate groups. America's war against itself became more intense when Trump compared the practices of US intelligence and media organizations to those of Nazi Germany in reaction to alleged Russian video tape of Trump in a compromising situation. Ironically, the so-called "Nazi" practices were attributed to the Obama-Clinton Democrats who have the institutional power to undermine the Republicans and persisted on the Russian hacking theme without ever providing evidence.

By comparing the US to the Third Reich, Trump expressed the deep divisions among the political elites while lending legitimacy to the criticism of America usually reserved for leftist critics arguing that the US has been sliding down the road of authoritarianism. If Noam Chomsky, for example, leveled the same criticism as Trump, it would have no significance beyond a small circle of those who follow Chomsky. When Trump compared his country to the Hitler's Third Reich, it afforded legitimacy to critics' arguments that indeed the US has authoritarian aspects, while preaching democracy to the world. Moreover, it revealed the depths of division in America that goes beyond politics and into the nature of the country's institutions failing both in social cohesion and political consensus.

By refusing to accept Trump as a legitimate president, perhaps because he lost the popular vote or because of email leaks through WIKILEAKS via Russia as a possible source, black Civil Rights leader and Georgia Congressman John Lewis contributed to de-legitimizing the new president in the eyes of the world. As a symbolic representative of the black community, Lewis was affirming that social exclusion and differentiation cannot be legitimized by a president who lost in the popular vote.

Behind the de-legitimization efforts, the media, social, academic, and financial elites naturally take sides, as do many ordinary people who watch and wonder if these clashes entail that the politics of consensus are a thing of the past and polarization the new reality. According to a Pew Research study, the partisanship and animosity between Republicans and Democrats has never been greater than in the 2016 presidential race. Each side sees the other as closed-minded, immoral, dishonest, unintelligent, and lazy, thus lacking trust in the other's ability to represent the social contract and lead the country.

To distract from the internal clash, the Democrats keep focusing on Russia, with their European Union allies doing likewise as the latter fear Trump may be less committed to the world order as they inherited it since the demise of the Soviet Bloc. Keeping with favorite theme of racism and xenophobia, Republicans focus on the "Clash of Civilizations" thesis as a means to distract from Russia and placate the domestic elites and rally popular support behind the flag. Neither "Clash of Civilizations" with Muslims as a target nor Russia with the evil Vladimir Putin and the corrupt oligarchs is enough to quell the culture clash; and neither is a credible substitute for addressing income inequality, lack of social justice and growing social exclusion and differentiation.

America at war with itself is unlikely to change toward the kind of consensus that existed in the early Cold War from Truman to Kennedy when the US was the undisputed superpower and upward social mobility kept the population hopeful about achieving the American Dream, at least for their children. In a world where power is shifting from the West to East Asia with a resurgent Russia despite Western containment policies and sanctions, the American elites are scrambling to preserve and expand their privileges while forging some kind of political consensus that will enable them to maintain the status quo. Against such efforts comes the reality that eight individuals, including Bill Gates, Warren Buffet, Jeff Bezos, Mark Zuckerberg, Larry Ellison and Michael Bloomberg, all Americans, own as much wealth as half of the world's population of 3.6 Billion.

The Nature of Division and Polarization in the US

The topic of culture clashes has been analyzed by hundreds of books and articles dealing with the deep divisions in American society. These are multifaceted divisions rooted in identity politics and class struggle politics of the last two centuries. However, the rise of social exclusion and differentiation is more evident today than at any time since the anti-war movement of the 1960s. From the Civil War to the Civil Rights Movement to the controversial election of 2000 and the equally contentious election of 2016, more scholarly works and journal articles have been devoted to growing rift in American society and what it entails. According to one poll at the beginning of 2016, 56% of Americans believed that their children would be worse off than they were. Another poll indicated that 81% were worse off in 2016 than in 2005. By contrast, only 20% are worse off in Sweden for the same time frame, indicative of income stagnation amid massive capital concentration. While these statistics clearly illustrate a policy intended toward greater social integration in Sweden, the exact opposite is the case for the US.

Polarization extends beyond the domain of income gap, encompassing geographic, racial, ethnic, religious, gender, and cultural issues and finding expression in the political parties and factions within factions of two major parties. Current polarized conditions are due to a general decline of the middle class and living standards among the working class at a time that identity politics—cultural, religious, racial, ethnic, and gender-based issues—is a necessary tool of the elites to prevent systemic institutional changes and maintain political consensus.

More resistant to the well-established bipartisan cooperation on key issues, including foreign policy consensus, armies of journalists, consultants, analysts, lobbyists, and academics promote the divisions of the political and socioeconomic elites. If the energy sector has vested interests in US-Russia cooperation, while the auto industry has vested interests in NAFTA, and high tech in East Asia, it is understandable that the respective corporate lobbies, journalists, consultants, think tanks, and of course politicians would disagree about foreign policy consensus. Not only is US economic power reflected in its corporate structure at a time of national economic decline, especially when taking into account that debt as percentage of GDP stands at 105 and rising, but the nature of the US economy in comparison to that of Asia speaks volumes about its dim prospects and continued socioeconomic and cultural polarization.

Whereas China is strengthening its infrastructure and that of countries where it invests from Asia and Africa to Latin America, it also has sound domestic foundations in the primary and secondary sectors of its economy. While China has created the Asian Infrastructure Investment Bank involved in nine major projects in 2016 and planning many more in the future, the US was busy trying to forge trading blocs in order to exclude China while securing better terms of trade and higher profits for multinational corporations, as the Trans-Pacific Partnership illustrates, assuming it is ever implemented.

Unlike China, the US relies heavily on the service sector, largely speculative and parasitic, along with the defense industry that is even more parasitic than the financial sector. One could argue that high tech, especially robotics and biotech are pioneering areas with a great deal of growth since the 1990s and good prospects for the US economy. While many of those operations are at home they are hardly exempt from globalization. That US companies are keeping at least $2.5 trillion overseas and refusing to repatriate it under the current tax rate speaks volumes of their lack of commitment to economic nationalism. This is one reason that high tech corporations backed globalization advocated by Clinton.

Despite Trump's tariff threats which are an admission of inability to compete by trade rule the US established, the outward trend of US capital and production will continue because of low labor costs and market share competition. One reason that the Trump administration is viewing globalization with skepticism and downplaying the World Economic Forum at Davos, Switzerland in January 2017 where globalists gather every year is because globalization favors the US less than China, Japan and other nations. For the first time ever, China will dominate the Davos conference a historically a Western-dominated affair.

Whereas China is a producing country enjoying a trade surplus, the US is a consumption-driven economy with a balance of payments deficit and rapidly rising public debt financed in part by the artificial value of the dollar as a reserve currency still widely used around the world for transactions such as oil trade. Reflationary economics, combined with infrastructural and defense spending intended to stimulate GDP growth will work short term but add to the national debt, a prospect that will result in even greater socioeconomic inequality and greater sociopolitical and cultural polarization.

Because countries producing about one-third of the world's output have pegged their currencies in dollars, and 39% of the world's debt is in dollars, the greenback has value much higher than any other hard currency. With its large productive capacity in all sectors of its economy and a large domestic consumer market, the US will remain economically strong. The question is for how long would the dollar continue to enjoy such a preeminent role; what happens when other reserve currencies become more competitive, and how long can the system sustain its viability under the weight of massive defense spending combined with a corporate welfare state. This inevitable development will further weaken the middle class and workers who feel increasingly marginalized but are confused about who is exactly to blame and how to fix the dysfunctional system.

Trump's inane slogan "Make America Great Again" by waving the magic wand of economic nationalism and flirtation with neo-isolationism reflect the realization of decline and a highly symbolic approach to stop the inevitable decline that enriches US-based multinational corporations at the expense of the socially excluded segments of society that make up the majority. His insistence that companies selling products in the US must manufacture them domestically is a tacit recognition of the corporate sector profiting to the detriment of the weakened middle class and workers. However, asking powerful multinational corporations to cooperate with economic nationalist policies without massive tax incentives, corporate subsidies, and a much more relaxed regulatory regime is unrealistic. While the president could follow some variation of a statist model, Wall Street and congress will never allow any deviation from neoliberal policies, and Trump has demonstrated his interest is to enrich his family and supporters.

Caught between policy contradictions and the realities of capitalism, the middle class and workers will pay the price because the government cannot find the money, unless it raises the national debt and slashes entitlements, for both the corporate welfare state and relaxed regulatory regime while maintaining a commitment to defense build up, higher living standards and protecting the environment. Just as the governor of Michigan opted for corporate givebacks at the expense of providing lead-contaminated water for Flint, the federal government will face similar choices and it will opt for corporate tax breaks, corporate subsidies, and privatization schemes that transfer income from the public sector to the private.

The growing absence of political consensus and the intense competition of the elites to influence policy has swept away the masses and divided them politically, ideologically, culturally, geographically and demographically and unable to grasp why there must be perpetual social exclusion and differentiation if the economy is expanding as evidenced by the GDP and stock market. Amid this political-ideological-cultural war in which America is engaged, it is ironic that establishment Democrats are not fighting their opponents from a leftist position associated with FDR's New Deal social safety net across the board with a strong central government role in the economy, but cling to identity politics—gay rights, environmentalists, blacks, Hispanics, women, etc. Trying to out-Republican Rockefeller Republicans who have more in common with the Cold War anti-Russia neoliberal Democrats than they do with the populist extreme right wing illustrates the bankruptcy of the Democrat Party as a realistic vehicle to social integration.

Is Secession a Possibility? In case of Secession, what would be its impact on the dollar and trade?

By 2016, the majority of Americans were angry and dissatisfied with their government led by a neoliberal Cold War Democrat President Obama whose actions did not match his rhetoric when it came to social justice and economic opportunity for all. Two weeks before the presidential election of 2016, a survey indicated that the nation was sharply divided on nearly everything from race relations to health care. The majority of people, 20% more than in 2012, believed the country was headed in the wrong direction and blamed the establishment Democrats and Republicans.

Polarization was evident when considering evangelical Protestants who associated America's glory with the Eisenhower administration, an era when institutionalized racism was legal and witch hunts against dissidents entailed absolute conformity in a country that called itself a democracy and castigated totalitarian Russia. Many populist conservatives that voted Trump are not bothered if their president violates the constitution and goes above the law to crush all enemies foreign and domestic, from ISIS in Iraq to illegal aliens and Black Lives Matter in the inner cities. In short, if authoritarianism is what it takes for social integration, then so be it, as far as the populist right wing is concerned. That populist conservatives lump together jihadists, illegal aliens, and minority activists speaks volumes of deep-seated cultural, political and institutional racism.

Beyond the obvious socioeconomic divisions that tend to be much more evident in southern states and rural areas, coastal states are enjoying higher living standards than the rest of the country and are culturally very different from most states except the larger Midwestern and even some large southern cities. The "Red-state" (Republican) vs. "Blue-state" (Democrat) divide transcends class and reflects more of a cultural and ideological chasm that reflects historic societal conditioning. Although it is true that the social, cultural, religious, financial, and political elites have shaped the ideological/cultural chasm largely to suppress class solidarity which poses a threat to capitalism, this divide is deeply rooted in American history layered with the experiences of the dominant white Western European culture as hegemonic subordinating all others.

As a political tool of rallying support behind the flag, shifting blame to external enemies has limited staying power, although the US did very well using Communism for half a century to achieve a domestic and international political consensus. Although large segments of the population feel excluded by the institutional structure, indoctrination has them convinced that enemies du jour are to blame, whether they are Russian and WIKILEAKS hackers, illegal immigrants, Muslims, the Chinese, etc. According to Pew Research public opinion data, the US did not become divided in 2016 as a result of the general election. The divisions in fact predate 9/11 and become sharper with the ideological/political gap widening as the income gap widened after the great recession of 2008. The decline in living standards follows a corresponding rise in the phenomenon of culture clashes and various socially excluded and differentiated groups seeking integration by different political means.

Considering the US progressive tradition was limited to the trade union movement from the late 19trh century until the Great

Depression but thoroughly co-opted, and considering the women's movement along with all other identity politics issues were also co-opted by the Democrat Party, there is no historical tradition of an effective progressive grassroots movement that takes under its umbrella all socially excluded and differentiated groups. Given this reality people turn to the right when a populist extreme right wing demagogue like Trump comes along and promises to restore the American Dream, although in practice will deliver more wealth concentration that will lead to even lower social integration levels than what he inherited.

Is Secession a Good Idea? Would liberal California or conservative Texas be better off as breakaway Republics?

Considering the polarizing societal conditions, one could imagine how perpetual division, even secession may enter the public discourse. Secession is a deep-seated fear or wish on the part of some Americans who see that country geographically, ideologically, politically, racially, ethnically and culturally divided. It is true that southern states do not reflect the values or lifestyles of the coastal states. It is equally true that the smaller less populated southern states enjoy as many votes in the senate as the larger coastal states, thus determining the national agenda for the majority of the population. Does such a system reflect the will of the people, the social contract, or is it simply a reflection of states' rights mentality that had relevance during the pre-Civil War slave era?

Secession was tried in the 1860s and failed miserably despite the considerable confidence of the southern elites who believed that their interests were better served by closer integration with England than the northern states. The secession movement that resulted in the Civil War suggests that secession is beyond the realm of possibility. Of course, people understand politics on the basis of their educational level, their family and local influences, their religious and ideological-political leanings, as well as cultural conditioning.

Rural Mississippi populist Republicans who link their identity to the Christian faith view New York Democrats as leftist atheists interested in destroying cherished southern traditions and values. In such case, the individual subordinates material self interest to religious faith and culture, as Samuel Huntington argued in "Clash of Civilizations" referring to a Middle East-West conflict rather than a domestic culture clash. Conservatives are spending billions of dollars every year trying to convince the masses to disregard their material self interests and focus on religion, cherished traditions, and loyalty to the nation, even if that means that every year their living standards decline and their prospects and those of their children for social integration diminish.

Conclusions

Not just the mass anti-Trump-inauguration demonstrations estimated at more than 200,000 people, but the media wars, social media and mainstream media "fake news," the political elites' wars, the struggle for the country's direction either toward a more authoritarian course or a liberal bourgeois based on pluralism, all provide a glimpse of a polarized society where social integration is the presumptive theoretical goal but exclusion and differentiation are realities. Although dialogue about the issues concerning the lives of the middle class and working people raises conflict in a capitalist society, the question is to what degree and how do the bourgeois political parties deal with social integration to achieve political consensus.

Under an imaginary scenario of secession, the cultural elites and some people on either side of the cultural divide would be happy if they were not bound by the federal government pursuing an ideological and political agenda with which they disagree sharply. Clearly, there is an ideological, political and cultural chasm between Texas and California, at so many levels, despite similarities especially in the larger cities of both states. It is also the case that while in many southern and rural areas there is convergence of religious dogma and conservative political ideology.

States have a great deal in common and would not give up the safety and security of the federal umbrella which makes possible US global reach partly because it has military bases around the world, military alliances, and the strong dollar as a reserve currency that is overvalued to the benefit of those holding it. Unless their privileges are taken from them by force as has been the case in revolutions, financial elites always manage to protect, preserve and expand their interests by backing the political status quo even if they have to reform it with a more progressive agenda, or support authoritarian policies, whichever side manages to forge a better popular consensus.

The reality of the well-integrated economy with global ties takes precedent over all other issues. California and Texas have economies largely in the primary sector of production but also in banking and high tech. This means that they need markets beyond their state borders and beyond US borders. Not just the costs of running an independent nation-state with sovereign currency, trade and investment policy that is in line with international organizations such as the WTO, World Bank, IMF, but also the reality of a mobile work force would complicate matters and make the breakaway states less competitive.

In the end, the political, ideological and cultural benefits would be so minor to the breakaway states, and economic costs so high that they would rejoin the union even if they were given the freedom to form their own nation. There is strength in unity and weakness in division. However, human beings are indeed irrational and material interests are not their only motivating factor in political choices. Indoctrinated by "Manifest Destiny" ideology and the American Dream of achieving greatness again even by association with the nation-state, people will sacrifice self-interest as they perceive it so they may satisfy their illusions such as identity with the militarily strong nation.

One possible scenario for the future of the US amid rapidly changing demographics is that it may resemble some aspects of post-Mandela South Africa. South African blacks have entered the political arena and government bureaucracy, they enjoy political rights and in theory equal protection under the law, but the economy and the entire institutional structure is designed to serve the white capitalist minority. As much as the US criticizes Russia for its authoritarianism and crony capitalism, is it that far off and is it not moving in that direction rather than the direction of the Scandinavian countries?

As the trend of massive wealth concentration under a corporate welfare state continues to erode the middle class and working class, the struggle against the tide of domestic and global history will keep America at war with itself and tilt it even more toward the road of authoritarianism and militarism after the next inevitable deep recession. Because popular expression of discontent lacks class solidarity owing to cultural divisions and identity politics in America, political leadership will not be under the umbrella of a leftist or even a center-left movement. America's future is an even more authoritarian regime with roots at the local and state levels financed by wealthy individuals like the Koch brothers among other likeminded billionaires, finding expression at the federal level with populist demagogues like Trump.

Jackie Robinson Changed Sports and the Nation

Justice B. Hill

Justice B. Hill is a sportswriter, and he teaches at the E.W. Scripps School of Journalism at Ohio University.

Jackie Robinson couldn't have known what Branch Rickey's "great experiment" would do to the socio-political landscape in America.

In fact, could anybody have known that putting Robinson, a black man, onto a baseball field with a team of white men would do for America what nothing else had done for race relations since the 1896 U.S. Supreme Court decision in *Plessy vs. Ferguson* legalized segregation?

"That's almost an impossible question to answer," said Robert Ruck, a senior lecturer at the University of Pittsburgh and an authority on black baseball. "I think that if Robinson's arrival in the Majors had been a chaotic social disaster, it would have made it more difficult for this country to change."

Historians like Ruck see Rickey's experiment, which opened the way for Robinson to break the color barrier with the Brooklyn Dodgers, as a trigger to a number of events that followed. It played a significant role, Ruck said, in fueling the move toward integration.

Yet perhaps no socio-political event in the first half of the 20th Century was as fraught with risk as this one.

"I don't see why a top-flight Negro ballplayer would be so anxious to play in the white leagues when he is doing so well in his own organization," Atlanta Journal sports editor Ed Danforth is quoted as saying at the time in historian Jules Tygiel's book "Baseball's Great Experiment: Jackie Robinson and His Legacy."

"Robinson Affected American Society," by Justice B. Hill, MLB Advanced Media, LP., April 14, 2007. Reprinted by Permission.

Even facing such intractable critics, black Americans and the black press had continued to call for integration—but not just in sports. They argued that democracy wasn't a black-white issue; their issue became one of equality.

How do people who had long been viewed as inferior prove they are an equal? They needed a defining moment, an event in history that so crystallized their equality that nobody could dispute the matter.

On April 15, 1947, Robinson provided that defining moment. He would have much to prove.

In agreeing to Rickey's terms for integrating the game, Robinson, a bright, educated man, had to douse the competitive fires that raged inside him. He realized that Rickey had almost asked the impossible. It might have been easier altogether if Rickey had asked Robinson to stop breathing.

For how could he put his emotions in mothballs?

But Robinson knew that he must corral his rage for Rickey's experiment to succeed. Historians said the late '40s weren't the time for militancy, not if meaningful progress in race relations were to be made in America.

"Robinson created a sort of picture that all society should be integrated," said Titus Brown, a professor of history and African-American Studies at Florida A&M University. "That's why we could see a shifting and changing in society in the mid-1950s."

The success of the experiment put segregation under society's microscope, Brown said. It forced people to take a different look at race in America.

"Breaking the color barrier did say, 'Maybe it's not so bad that you can have an African-American athlete participate in the so-called American sport," Brown said. "I think people started to rethink it after they saw Robinson."

He suggested that President Harry S Truman's 1948 decree that integrated the Armed Forces might have been an outgrowth of the successful desegregation of baseball. Ruck said Truman, perhaps emboldened by Robinson, seemed to sense that, in an election year, he had plenty to gain from opening opportunities to blacks.

"It seems to me," Ruck said, "that when something happens in one area of American life and it happens smoothly—maybe not from Jackie's point of view, because he had to deal with a lot—then that just makes it easy for further change.

"In subtle, subconscious ways, it makes it easier for white people to accept black people and to hire black people in positions they had not been hired before."

Robinson also made it easier for blacks to stoke the fires for full equality. After Truman's decree in '48, the quest for equal rights gathered momentum.

Within a decade, the doctrine of "separate but equal," which had governed race relations in the United States since the dawn of the 1900s, gave way to the U.S. Supreme Court decision in *Brown vs. the Board of Education of Topeka* in 1954, which struck down one of the legal barriers that blacks had to hurdle.

Other changes would soon follow, and the civil rights movement quickened its pace from there as black stars like Monte Irvin, Larry Doby, Willie Mays and Don Newcombe continued to prove that they could compete and play alongside white ballplayers.

"If you break down barriers in one field, it directly impacts others, particularly economic, political and social," said Julius Thompson, a professor of history and black studies at the University of Missouri. "So for me, it had implications in all these other areas in advancing civil rights and general human rights in the United States and other countries."

Yet all of these socio-political advances came with struggles, Ruck said. The advances were never straightforward; they were never uniform across American society.

Ruck, Thompson and Brown said Major League Baseball, thanks to Robinson, had a profound influence on putting those changes in motion.

"But you've got to remember that Robinson was an exceptional player," Brown said. "So if he had been a failure, it would have impacted the way people viewed blacks, especially in the arena of baseball."

Baseball Helps Us Understand Ourselves

William McKenzie and Talmage Boston

William Mckenzie is a former columnist for the Dallas Morning News *and current editorial director of the Bush Institute. Talmage Boston is the author of* 1939: Baseball's Tipping Point *and* Baseball and the Baby Boomer.

> *"This is the last pure place where Americans dream. This is the last great arena, the last green arena, where everybody can learn lessons of life."*
>
> *—A. Bartlett Giamatti,*
> *former Commissioner of*
> *Major League Baseball*

For more than a century, baseball has been labeled the "national pastime." American youths have taken to Little League parks and baseball diamonds for generations. The song "Take Me Out to the Ballgame" is part of American lore. Writers have rhapsodized about the game in their novels and histories while movie studios have released blockbuster films like *Field of Dreams*, *A League of Their Own and Moneyball.*

Nevertheless, as the 2015 baseball season began, the national pastime was faced with a slew of questions about its future. Perceived problems with the game went to the core of baseball's sustainability, as the Washington Post's Marc Fisher wrote:

> "Baseball has lived for the better part of a century on its unchanging character, its role as a bond between generations,

"Why Baseball Matters—Still" by William McKenzie and Talmage Boston, George W. Bush Presidential Center. Reprinted by Permission.

its identity as a quintessentially American game that features a one-on-one faceoff of individual skills tucked inside a team sport. Can a game with deliberation and anticipation at its heart thrive in a society revved up for nonstop action and scoring?"

Indeed, baseball's deliberate pace in a high-speed world is one of the sport's major challenges.

Before rule changes took effect this season to speed up play, the game had been taking longer at a time when Americans have been moving at an increasingly frenetic rate at almost every juncture of their lives. On average, games lasted three hours and two minutes in 2014, up from two hours and 33 minutes in 1981.

The slower pace was accompanied by fewer runs being scored, including fewer home runs, always a fan favorite. In 2014, major league teams scored about 5,000 fewer runs than in 2000 and about 1,500 fewer homers were hit. The lack of offensive spark became jarring to Americans accustomed to bells-and-whistles entertainment.

The sport faced other realities as well.

Upon Derek Jeter's retirement at the end of the 2014 season, baseball had few bona-fide superstars capable of drawing national attention to the game. No player in 2015 can compare in popularity with the glory days of Babe Ruth, Lou Gehrig, Joe DiMaggio, Mickey Mantle and Willie Mays, or, in more recent times, Johnny Bench, Hank Aaron, Nolan Ryan and Cal Ripken.

In proof of this point, no baseball players were listed among the 30 favorite sports figures in ESPN's most recent survey of American youths.

Like much else in American life, competition matters. Baseball is in the marketplace with other sports and entertainment options. "We sell competition," Major League Baseball Commissioner Rob Manfred told a Bush Center forum as the season began. Alas, all sports sell competition.

Attracting fans to the park is only part of the challenge. Television contracts and merchandise sales depend, in part, upon the fan appeal of the players on the field. Absent today's generation of players and fans passing their love of the game on to a new generation, baseball will survive as the national pastime in name only.

Local communities and their teams in smaller media markets have become baseball's biggest success stories. They have risen as big city teams with national followings, like the New York Yankees and Los Angeles Dodgers, have underperformed in recent years. There is a downside, however, to the rise of smaller-market teams. The 2014 World Series between the San Francisco Giants and Kansas City Royals went seven games, but it was the lowest-rated Fall Classic ever in the Nielsen ratings.

In spite of these challenges, baseball maintains that enduring connection with America. The sport even extends into the life of the Oval Office.

This symbiotic relationship gives baseball a unique place in our national life. The game still matters because through baseball we gain insight into our own national issues. Baseball helps us understand ourselves.

Baseball, Immigration, and the Quest for Freedom

Immigration has been a major story in America over the last two decades, but a big force in baseball longer than that. With each succeeding decade, the game has become more of a global enterprise and shows how open arms to people beyond America's shores can enhance an operation. Major league games are now routinely broadcast in other languages and the international media, particularly from Japan and the Far East, send reporters to cover games from spring training through the World Series.

What's more, Major League Baseball reports that 230 out of the game's 868 players on rosters at the start of the 2015 season were born outside the United States. This year, the Texas Rangers have 15 players from eight countries and territories. That is the most of any club for the second consecutive year, prompting the Dallas Morning News' Gerry Fraley to call the Rangers "a team of nations."

The thorough integration of the game did not just happen. For many years, baseball scouts have actively evaluated young talent from the Dominican Republic to Venezuela to Japan to Australia.

The growth in players from Latin America and the Caribbean has arguably been the most transformational element of the game since the 1980s. Beginning in the 1950s, players like Minnie Minoso from Cuba and Roberto Clemente from Puerto Rico made it to the major leagues and became stars.

Yet Minoso and Clemente were among the few Latino players during the Fifties and Sixties. Today, Latin superstars have become a dominant force. The 2015 season began with 83 major league players from the Dominican Republic alone.

Baseball long had been a popular sport in the Caribbean and Latin America. Yet baseball academies that major league teams built and staffed soon became a key step toward the big leagues. They welcomed the most talented Latin American players, even from closed societies like Venezuela. This season, 65 Venezuelans started the year in the major leagues.

Teams have not operated academies in Cuba, but 18 Cuban were on rosters as this year began. The list included Yasiel Puig, the Los Angeles Dodgers outfielder. His harrowing story of escape from Cuba includes being raced to Mexico on a cigarette boat, being held in a Mexico motel at the mercy of human smugglers and eventually winding up a Dodger in June 2012.

Puig is not the only player to escape oppression through baseball. Washington Nationals catcher Wilson Ramos made it out of Venezuela through his baseball prowess, but kept returning home after each season. After being kidnapped in Venezuela while visiting his mother in 2011, he eventually decided to seek a U.S. green card. "It's not easy to be with a bodyguard all the time," Ramos told the *Wall Street Journal.* "It's not the life you want to live."

Indeed, the desire to be free extends beyond the political world. Athletes seek open societies, just like those who are imprisoned for their beliefs. When players like Puig and Ramos take to the field in a major league ballpark, they personify the human search for freedom and the opportunity to maximize one's potential.

Of course, the baseball diamond reflected the quest for freedom and equal rights long before players suffering oppression abroad came to the U.S.

With his 1947 trailblazing entry into the major leagues, Jackie Robinson became a leading figure in the American civil rights movement. When the Brooklyn Dodgers' star infielder could finally play on the same team as white players, stay in their hotels, and eat at their same restaurants, America took a huge step away from its stained past. Baseball became integrated before the American military did, and 17 years before the Civil Rights Act passed in 1964.

Robinson's breakthrough was long in coming. The Negro Leagues existed in the early and middle parts of the last century. Stars like Josh Gibson, Buck Leonard, and Oscar Charles were denied the opportunity to play in the major leagues during their careers, even though they more than held their own in off-season exhibition games against All-Star teams made up of MLB's best players.

This dual segregated system provided a place for talented players of both races to showcase their skills. Yet it perpetuated the image of two "separate but equal" Americas, which, in fact, were not at all equal in salaries, travel, and playing conditions. The lack of full opportunity for players of all colors robbed the major leagues of great talent for many decades.

Strategic thinking by baseball's leaders was required to open the path to racial equality and free market opportunity, just as strategists like Dr. Martin Luther King, Jr. and Thurgood Marshall planned the social and legal path to equal opportunity for African-Americans in the 1950s.

Branch Rickey played the most important strategist role in integrating professional baseball, earning him the title of baseball's "Great Emancipator." Rickey was the Dodgers president who signed Jackie Robinson and partnered with him in breaking MLB's color barrier. He did not sign Robinson simply because he believed it was the morally correct thing to do. Rickey also did it because having Robinson in his lineup made the Dodgers a better ballclub. In Robinson's first year in Brooklyn, he led the team to the National League pennant and won Rookie of the Year honors.

As with the larger national struggle for civil rights, the integration of baseball did not come easily or without ugly incidents. But it did come, and the game benefited from the change. So did America.

Unfortunately, the participation of African-American ballplayers has declined dramatically in recent years. Baseball is a hard sport to play without a field, which can be hard to find in America's inner cities or poorer neighborhoods. Major League Baseball has tried to deal with this problem by providing funding to build fields in neighborhoods that lack them.

This may be one of the game's most pressing challenges, and, in many respects, it mirrors the challenge that urban leaders across America face: How can they rebuild their inner cities and neglected neighborhoods?

Baseball and Economics

Nowhere does baseball mirror American life more than in economics. This is true whether the issue is management/labor tension, free agency and the atomization of the workforce, or managing a complex organization.

The most serious management/labor dispute ended the 1994 season. As president, Bill Clinton tried to keep the game from finishing in a strike. He convened both sides at the White House, met with negotiators, and even tried to get Congress to impose binding arbitration. Unfortunately, his efforts did not succeed. The sides could not resolve their differences, and the season ended bitterly with the cancellation of the World Series.

The right of players to leave their existing teams and sign as free agents with other clubs constituted its own protracted, disputed struggle from the 1970s through the mid-1990s. Players eventually won the right to market their services to the team of their choice, thanks in part to Curt Flood, the St. Louis Cardinal star outfielder who rejected a trade to the Philadelphia Phillies in 1969. He opposed the trade because he thought baseball's reserve clause gave team owners too much control over ballplayers' economic freedom and prevented them from becoming free agents.

Flood fought his case all the way to the U.S. Supreme Court, but ultimately lost. His case did galvanize other players and, by the middle 1970s, the sport was on its way to allowing free agency for veteran players.

At the same time baseball was figuring out free agency, the American workforce was about to experience its own major shift. The technology revolution would soon make employees more individualized units of production. Like baseball's free agents signing with three or four franchises during their careers, employees found themselves on paths to multiple jobs during their working years. No longer would they be tethered to a single employer for a lifetime.

For players, free agency meant a rapid escalation in salaries. They were able to use the marketplace to get a better deal. Perhaps the most eye-striking contrast with today's players is the salary of the legendary Hank Aaron, who toppled Babe Ruth's career home run record in 1973. Aaron earned at most an annual salary of $250,000, and it came at the end of his standout career.

In 2015, the average salary of a major league player is more than $4 million and guaranteed contracts in excess of $100 million over several years is not unusual. Even when adjusted for inflation, Aaron's highest annual salary was less than $1 million in today's dollars.

Eye-popping salaries have rewarded some athletes with economic security for life, though they have also created the game's own wealth gap. The 2015 Texas Rangers' highest-paid player, Prince Fielder, will make $24 million this season, while about half of his teammates will receive the guaranteed minimum MLB salary of $500,000.

High-dollar salaries also make the economics of running a big league team challenging, causing the Los Angeles Dodger and Texas Rangers to recently go through reorganization proceedings in bankruptcy court.

Regardless of their size, modern ballplayers' salaries are a product of supply-and-demand, the ultimate market principle. The 30 MLB clubs carry rosters with 25 players each. (Teams are allowed 40-man rosters late in each season.) Given the vast number of ballplayers around the world, and the reality of market economics, those who make it to the big leagues and become accomplished stars there, naturally draw high salaries.

With increased technology, baseball has become a more sophisticated game in the Information Age. Each new year bring new data and performance measurements that drive decisions about lineups, field positioning, and pitching matchups. This is no different from how waves of data drive decision-making in such fields as finance, medicine and education.

Moneyball, Michael Lewis' best-seller about the modern game, explained how number-crunching professionals increasingly influence baseball. With each passing year, general managers, scouts, and managers collect and then use more information about the tendencies of their own players as well of players on opposing teams. As a manager, Tony LaRussa made full use of every piece of computerized information to micromanage his Oakland Athletics and St. Louis Cardinals to World Series championships.

Yet long before technology helped baseball develop sophisticated metrics, managers constantly innovated and were their own dynamic market force.

Casey Stengel implemented the platoon system of creating lineups, recognizing that left-handed batters typically succeed more often when facing right-handed pitchers, and vice versa. Connie Mack began the practice of analyzing hitters' weaknesses and then getting pitchers to take advantage of those weaknesses. Gene Mauch got his pitchers to vary their delivery in order to prevent base runners from getting too big of a lead before attempting to steal a base.

So, yes, baseball is a game and an athletic contest, but it also has provided a snapshot into the forces at play in a market economy. For that reason alone, the sport demands our attention.

Baseball and Leadership

The art of leadership is another way the sport demands our attention. Beyond the data-driven dugout decisions, or even the manager simply playing a hunch, there is the operation of Major League Baseball itself.

This season, Rob Manfred became the first new commissioner in more than 20 years. A Little Leaguer in childhood, Manfred had a successful legal career before joining MLB in 1998 as an executive and working closely in several positions under his predecessor Bud Selig.

Selig came into baseball as owner of the Milwaukee Braves and later the Milwaukee Brewers. In 1992, he became commissioner and enjoyed a long and successful tenure. That was largely due to his capacity to build consensus among MLB's owners, especially as they faced such crises as the use of steroids.

Through the challenges, Selig lived on the phone not only with owners, but also with all of the game's constituents. His approach allowed him to find the sweet-spot on controversial issues. Like a shrewd legislative leader, Selig knew when he had the votes to bring up a major decision.

Selig's consensus-oriented style produced results, even when his final decisions generated controversy. His greatest achievements included growing the game's popularity internationally, substantially increasing revenues for all clubs, and averting labor/management breakdowns.

Baseball's intersection with the nation's political leaders creates its own deep connection with Americans. There is the traditional presidential toss of the first pitch on Opening Day. More important than following tradition, presidents have recognized that the game can rally the country in times of crisis.

Americans were stunned by the terrorist attacks that occurred on September 11, 2001. New York City especially reeled in the emotional turmoil.

When President George W. Bush strode to the mound at Yankee Stadium on October 30, 2001 to deliver the first pitch in Game Three of the 2001 World Series, a perfect strike at that, the chants of "U-S-A, U-S-A" that reverberated through that venerable stadium echoed across the land and the world. The message was delivered: America may have been bloodied, but it was not bowed.

Franklin Roosevelt also understood the symbolism of baseball. Shortly after the attack on Pearl Harbor on December 7, 1941, he wrote the famous "Green Letter," asking that baseball executives not cancel the upcoming 1942 season. He knew that families worried about their young soldiers at war could alleviate their stress and draw at least some pleasure from taking trips to the ballpark or simply gathering around the radio to hear a broadcast.

Richard Nixon grasped baseball's importance, too. After his motorcade was stoned in Venezuela while he served as Dwight Eisenhower's vice president, he asked the State Department to send big league players to the country on a goodwill mission. "The tour did more to clear the atmosphere than a dozen top-echelon conferences," a former U.S. ambassador to Venezuela later said.

Of course, baseball inculcates leadership skills far beyond the presidential level. The sport starts early training youth as leaders through Little League, the YMCA and other leagues. The focus goes beyond developing athletic skills to creating situations where children can work together as a team and develop sportsmanship.

Baseball and the Military

During World War II and the Korean War, Americans saw star players trade in their teams' uniforms for the military uniforms of the United States. Promising careers were interrupted for service to the nation.

- After serving in World War II, Ted Williams then flew 39 missions in the Korean War. His plane got hit on several flights, including one strike that forced him to land his burning plane on a flight deck. Fellow Marine aviator John Glenn thought of the great Williams most of all as a pilot. "Much as I appreciate baseball," Glenn said, "Ted to me will always be a Marine fighter pilot."

- Bob Feller, the Cleveland Indians Hall of Famer, volunteered for duty on the day after Pearl Harbor, and spent more than two years as chief of an anti-aircraft gun crew on a battleship.
- Lou Brissie, subject of *The Corporal Was a Pitcher*, begged that his leg not be amputated after being severely injured in Italy during World War II. He not only kept his leg, but recovered sufficiently to become an All Star pitcher in 1949.
- Sadly, not all baseball players survived their wartime service. Harry O'Neill was among them, dying in the battle for Iwo Jima.

Fast forward to today, baseball remains connected to those who serve their country in the military. Veterans who fought in Iraq and Afghanistan face challenges as they move from the military into civilian life.

Traumatic injuries create their own special problems. Veterans coping with a lost limb or post-traumatic stress often need a variety of medical and social services to complete their reentries.

To their credit, teams like the New York Mets have stepped into the breach. Mets' Chairman and CEO Fred Wilpon helped create the Welcome Back Veterans organization, which Major League Baseball significantly supports, to provide veterans with quality medical care.

The organization particularly assists veterans who struggle with post-traumatic stress. Welcome Back Veterans, along with partners, funds research into PTS at hospitals in New York, Massachusetts, Michigan, Georgia, California, North Carolina and Illinois. The ultimate aim is to create Centers of Excellence that provide veterans the best possible treatment for post-traumatic stress.

The Mets also have implemented Military Mondays to honor individual veterans as well as provide veterans discounted tickets.

Many other major league teams likewise offer current military personnel and returning veterans discounted tickets.

Efforts like these symbolize the relationship between baseball and American society, though they go beyond symbolism. They open the door back into a world of family, community, and employment for returning service members. At the same time, they open the door back into the national pastime for returning veterans.

Baseball's Road Ahead

This unique relationship with American society is one of baseball's strengths. Yet too many pressures exist to assume this connection will continue without significant attention and nurturing.

Baseball faces the same pressure that news organizations, religious institutions, and even late-night comedians encounter: how to engage young Americans. Declining numbers illustrate baseball's problem. The *Wall Street Journal* recently reported that the number of American youths age seven to 17 playing in organized baseball leagues declined from 8.8 million in 2000 to 5.3 million in 2013.

Specialized sports are part of the problem. Children lock into one sport at an early age and don't play other sports in an organized way.

Still, the game benefits from being played every day for more than half the year. The sport is part of the American rhythm, as Roger Kahn captured in *The Boys of Summer*. Each summer, seven days a week, baseball fans listen to games on TV and radio, check their newspapers and favorite websites for the latest box scores and stay abreast of who's injured, who's not, who's hot, who's cold, who got traded and who stayed behind.

Along with those rhythms, baseball embeds itself into the American mind through the power of storytelling. Pulitzer Prize-winning historian Doris Kearns Goodwin has ascribed her ability to write a narrative from her childhood days listening to the Brooklyn Dodgers on the radio. The ballgames revealed to her that each game has a beginning, a middle and an end, making the perfect vehicles for storytelling.

Most games in the 1950s were played during the day, so the young Goodwin would keep score and report to her father when he got home all the details of that day's game. "He made me feel I was telling him a fabulous story," Goodwin once said. "It makes you think there's something magic about history to keep your father's attention."

Today, baseball's stories are told in new ways. MLB's popular At Bat app. ESPN's *Baseball Tonight*. You Tube. They are among the many modern opportunities to follow the sport.

Ballplayers themselves tell wonderful stories, many colorful, many humorous. Through those stories, we learn how ordinary individuals find ways to perform extraordinary feats. Unlike many sports, baseball does not require an outsized physique. One of the greatest of all, Willie Mays, stood only 5'10" and weighed 170 pounds.

Of course, families themselves hand down their own baseball stories. Grandparents regale grandchildren with tales of their favorite players from old, while grandchildren bring grandparents up to date on what all the new categories of statistics mean. Similarly, generations of families attend games together. And parents in 2015 delight in playing catch with their children just like parents and children did in 1915.

Economics. Leadership. Immigration. The quest for freedom. Equal rights. The Information Age. Veterans. Even storytelling. These are among the ways in which this sport connects with Americans at a deep level. They also are why baseball still matters. The game provides a lens into our very society and remains one of America's most reliable means of connecting generations.

Jackie Robinson Broke the Color Barrier, But People of Color Are Still at Risk

Sanford Jay Rosen

Sanford Jay Rosen is the founding partner of Rosen Bien Galvan & Grunfeld LLP, where he focuses on constitutional and civil rights law. Rosen has argued before the U.S. Supreme Court five times.

Recently I watched "The Jackie Robinson Story" ("TJRS") (1950) (staring Jackie Robinson as himself) and "42" (2013) back to back. They tell the story of how Robinson broke the color barrier in professional baseball and changed race relations in America.

Watching the movies, I thought about some of the bad and terrible still imbedded in race in America. In June, five of the nine members of the Supreme Court put the voting rights of African Americans and other minorities seriously at risk for the first time since enactment of the Voting Rights Act in 1965. African Americans remain subject to profiling and targeting by vigilantes and police, as demonstrated by the killings of Trayvon Martin in Sanford, Florida and Oscar Grant in Oakland, California. Young African American men over-populate our prisons and death rows disproportionately to their numbers in the general population.

The movies transported me to 1947, when I was nine, living in Brooklyn and, like everyone I knew, a committed Brooklyn Dodgers fan. One day I was having my hair cut. A bunch of the barbers and customers talk about how Dixie Walker (the Dodgers right fielder and then one of my heroes) was leaving the team because Robinson was joining it. For years, I wondered what that was about.

My family was committed to the "Jackie Robinson Dodgers." When we listened to games on the radio, if Robinson got a hit, stole a base, or made a great play, my mother would exclaim: "That's

"Jackie Robinson and Race in America, Then and Now: A Tale of Two Movies," by Sanford Jay Rosen, TheHuffingtonPost.com, Inc., October 14, 2013. Reprinted by Permission.

my boy." She meant no offense and none would have been taken, which is apparent in TJRS.

TJRS and "42" tell the same story, and plumb the depths of race hatred and segregation. Both dramatize incidents, often the same ones. But, they use different words, tones and colors that inform us about race in America in 1950 (the year TJRS was released), and now 63 years later in 2013 (when "42" was released).

TJRS soft peddles the darkest sides of racism and "Jim Crow," the web of segregation laws and practices enacted and implemented, following the Civil War and the end of Reconstruction, still in place well into the 1960's. Branch Rickey, who brought Robinson to the Dodgers, refers to him as "boy" without even a hint that it was demeaning; the words "nigger" and "shine" are used only once each. Images of segregated buses, restaurants and hotels, and risks of violence are muted. The 1950 film even has comic relief principally in the antics of a diminutive player called "Shorty."

TJRS ends with Robinson addressing Congress, prophetically imagining "a country where every child has the opportunity to become President."

Although "42" is upbeat, there is nothing funny, light or muted in it about bigotry, segregation, and threats of violence. It shows racism for what it is—raw, ugly and dangerous. "42" pushes in our faces stark images of segregated hotels, public rest rooms, public transportation, the unlimited power minor white functionaries had over African Americans, and ever present risks of violence. It includes among its brutal images an extended dramatization of Phillies manager Ben Chapman repeatedly yelling "nigger" and other hateful epithets at Robinson.

TJRS showed segregation and racism to white northern audiences in a lazy way without starkly displaying its brutality, probably because in 1950, lynching's and the grossest kinds of Jim Crow mostly were relegated to the South. Nothing much had happened to challenge everyday segregation. President Truman had issued an order integrating the military in 1948, but only after early defeats in Korea did the command structure systematically begin implementing the order. And those changes took place in the separate world of the military.

Then along comes the 1954 Brown school desegregation decision. It is followed in 1957 and 1958 by images on television of hateful violent white mobs terrorizing nine black high school students who desegregated Little Rock Central High School, which was followed in the 1960's by the Freedom Summers complete with freedom riders and Southern blacks brutalized by clubs, police dogs, fire hoses and Klan murders. The nation was galvanized to end segregation.

"42" shows the images of segregation's everyday brutality and its violence in a way that TJRS could not, because they had not yet caught most white northerners' eyes when TJRS was shot. "42" also shows more violent imagery of segregation and racism because today we can think about them as mostly "history"—i.e., safely remote in time.

Yet, although not constantly in our faces, racism and discrimination remain close to the surface, giving me pause personally and as a citizen.

Racism is again so soft-focus that the Supreme Court got away with gutting the 1965 Voting Rights Act. Section 4 and Section 5 of the Act required several southern states, and parts of other states, including my adopted home state of California, to pre-clear with the U.S. Department of Justice or federal courts any changes in their laws affecting voting due to those jurisdictions' long history of interfering with African Americans' or Latinos' right to vote. It was reenacted overwhelmingly by Congress and signed by President George W. Bush in 2006. This June, a five person majority of the Supreme Court declared Section 4 unconstitutional on the grounds that the mountain of evidence on which the 2006 reenactment was based was stale and not linked to current African American voting patterns.

The center piece of the decision is epitomized by Chief Justice Roberts' observation that: "But history did not end in 1965." Of course not. However, even though African Americans and other minorities increasingly vote and capture political office in the States and jurisdictions that were subject to Sections 4 and 5 of the Voting Rights Act, not enough has changed since 1947, 1950, 1954 or 1965.

Republican-governed Texas, Mississippi, Alabama, North Carolina and Florida's immediate responses to the 2013 Voting Rights decision were to tighten voter eligibility standards, shorten voting times, and tighten voter identification requirements—to purge voting rolls of people suspected of not being eligible to vote. The brunt of these efforts demean and fall heavily on persons of color, most of whom are entitled to vote.

Both of the Jackie Robinson movies include scenes of Robinson at Spring training in 1946 with the Montreal Royals in Sanford, Florida. Sanford's police chief quashed Robinson's participation in practice games, because local law prohibited mixed race sporting events.

It is impossible not to think about volunteer watchman George Zimmerman's killing of Trayvon Martin in Sanford last year, and Zimmerman acquittal of murder and manslaughter. Almost surely, the unarmed young African American victim was racially profiled by the heavily armed Zimmerman, but that was not part of the proof at trial.

One of my sons-in-law is African American, and two of my grandchildren are beautiful mixed race or African American teenagers. My son-in-law has told me just a little of his experience with racial profiling. I have witnessed some of the thinly veiled reactions he and my daughter get to being a bi-racial couple, and similar reactions to my African American grandchildren. I cannot help but worry about how potentially unsafe and subject to racial bigotry they would be if they travel to Florida to visit relatives.

When I think about Oscar Grant's killing (adjudged involuntary manslaughter) by a white BART policeman at BART's Oakland, California Fruitvale station, I worry about my family's risks even in the progressive San Francisco Bay Area.

TJRS and "42" identify the essence of why people of color remain more at risk in America than Caucasians. TJRS includes a scene in which Clay Hopper, the manager of the Montreal Royals, asks Branch Rickey: "Do you really think he [Robinson] is a human being?"

In "42," Dodgers' manager Leo Durocher exhorts the Dodgers team shortly after Robinson joined it: "I do not care if the guy is yellow or black, or if he has stripes like a f**kin' zebra." As Durocher pungently says it, race and color need to be perceived by all as little more than curiosities, not characteristics that define a person's humanity.

Early TV Promoted Traditional Gender Roles and Family Structures

American Yawp

American Yawp is an open source textbook of American history edited by Joseph Locke and Ben Wright.

America's consumer economy reshaped how Americans experienced culture and shaped their identities. The Affluent Society gave Americans new experiences, new outlets, and new ways to understand and interact with one another.

"The American household is on the threshold of a revolution," the *New York Times* declared in August 1948. "The reason is television."[16] Presented to the American public at New York World's Fair in 1939, the commercialization of television in the United States lagged during the war year. In 1947, though, regular full-scale broadcasting became available to the public. Television was instantly popular, so much so that by early 1948 *Newsweek* reported that it was "catching on like a case of high-toned scarlet fever."[17] Indeed, between 1948 and 1955 close to two-thirds of the nation's households purchased a television set. By the end of the 1950s, 90 percent of American families had one and the average viewer was tuning in for almost 5 hours a day.[18]

The technological ability to transmit images via radio waves gave birth to television. Television borrowed radio's organizational structure, too. The big radio broadcasting companies, NBC, CBS, and ABC, used their technical expertise and capital reserves to conquer the airwaves. They acquired licenses to local stations and eliminated their few independent competitors. The Federal Communication Commission's (FCC) refusal to issue any new

"Gender and Culture in the Affluent Society," American Yawp, http://www.americanyawp.com/text/26-the-affluent-society/#V_Gender_and_Culture_in_the_Affluent_Society. Licensed Under CC BY-SA 4.0 International.

licenses between 1948 and 1955 was a de facto endorsement of the big three's stranglehold on the market.

In addition to replicating radio's organizational structure, television also looked to radio for content. Many of the early programs were adaptations of popular radio variety and comedy shows, including the *Ed Sullivan Show* and *Milton Berle's Texaco Star Theater*. These were accompanied by live plays, dramas, sports, and situation comedies. Due to the cost and difficulty of recording, most programs were broadcast live, forcing stations across the country to air shows at the same time. And since audiences had a limited number of channels to choose from, viewing experiences were broadly shared. Upwards of two thirds of television-owning households, for instance, watched popular shows such as *I Love Lucy*.

The limited number of channels and programs meant that networks selected programs that appealed to the widest possible audience to draw viewers and, more importantly, television's greatest financers: advertisers. By the mid-1950s, an hour of primetime programming cost about $150,000 (about $1.5 million in today's dollars) to produce. This proved too expensive for most commercial sponsors, who began turning to a joint financing model of 30-second spot ads. The commercial need to appeal to as many people as possible promoted the production of non-controversial shows aimed at the entire family. Programs such as *Father Knows Best* and *Leave it to Beaver* featured light topics, humor, and a guaranteed happy ending the whole family could enjoy.[19]

Television's broad appeal, however, was about more than money and entertainment. Shows of the 1950s, such as *Father Knows Best* and *I Love Lucy*, idealized the nuclear family, "traditional" gender roles, and white, middle-class domesticity. *Leave It to Beaver*, which became the prototypical example of the 1950s' television family, depicted its breadwinner-father and homemaker-mother guiding their children through life lessons. Such shows, and Cold War America more broadly, reinforced a popular consensus that such lifestyles were not only beneficial, but the most effective way to safeguard American prosperity against communist threats and social "deviancy."

Postwar prosperity facilitated, and in turn was supported by, the ongoing postwar baby boom. From 1946 to 1964, American fertility experienced an unprecedented spike. A century of declining birth rates abruptly reversed. Although popular memory credits the cause of the baby boom to the return of virile soldiers from battle, the real story is more nuanced. After years of economic depression families were now wealthy enough to support larger families and had homes large enough to accommodate them, while women married younger and American culture celebrated the ideal of a large, insular family.

Underlying this "reproductive consensus" was the new cult of professionalism that pervaded postwar American culture, including the professionalization of homemaking. Mothers and fathers alike flocked to the experts for their opinions on marriage, sexuality, and, most especially, child-rearing. Psychiatrists held an almost mythic status as people took their opinions and prescriptions, as well as their vocabulary, into their everyday life. Books like Dr. Spock's *Baby and Child Care* (1946) were diligently studied by women who took their careers as house-wife as just that: a career, complete with all the demands and professional trappings of job development and training. And since most women had multiple children roughly the same age as their neighbors' children, a cultural obsession with kids flourished throughout the decade. Women bore the brunt of this pressure, chided if they did not give enough of their time to the children—especially if it was because of a career—yet cautioned that spending too much time would lead to "Momism," producing "sissy" boys who would be incapable of contributing to society and extremely susceptible to the communist threat.

A new youth culture exploded in American popular culture. On the one hand, the anxieties of the atomic age hit America's youth particularly hard. Keenly aware of the discontent bubbling beneath the surface of the Affluent Society, many youth embraced rebellion. The 1955 film *Rebel Without a Cause* demonstrated the restlessness and emotional incertitude of the postwar generation raised in increasing affluence yet increasingly unsatisfied with their comfortable lives. At the same time, perhaps yearning for something beyond the "massification" of American culture yet having few other options to turn to beyond popular culture, American youth embraced rock 'n' roll. They listened to Little Richard, Buddy Holly, and especially Elvis Presley (whose sexually suggestive hip movements were judged subversive).

The popularity of rock and roll had not yet blossomed into the countercultural musical revolution of the coming decade, but it provided a magnet for teenage restlessness and rebellion. "Television and Elvis," the musician Bruce Springsteen would recollect, "gave us full access to a new language, a new form of communication, a new way of being, a new way of looking, a new way of thinking; about sex, about race, about identity, about life; a new way of being an American, a human being; and a new way of hearing music." American youth had seen so little of Elvis' energy and sensuality elsewhere in their culture. "Once Elvis came across the airwaves," Springsteen said, "once he was heard and seen in action, you could not put the genie back in the bottle. After that moment, there was yesterday, and there was today, and there was a red hot, rockabilly forging of a new tomorrow, before your very eyes."[20]

Other Americans took larger steps to reject the expected conformity of the Affluent Society. The writers and poets and musicians of the Beat Generation, disillusioned with capitalism, consumerism, and traditional gender roles, sought a deeper meaning in life. Beats traveled across the country, studied Eastern religions, and experimented with drugs and sex and art.

Behind the scenes, Americans were challenging sexual mores. The gay rights movement, for instance, stretched back into the Affluent Society. While the country proclaimed homosexuality a mental disorder, gay men established the Mattachine Society in Los Angeles and gay women formed the Daughters of Bilitis in

San Francisco as support groups. They held meetings, distributed literature, provided legal and counseling services, and formed chapters across the country. Much of their work, however, remained secretive because homosexuals risked arrest and abuse, if discovered.[21]

Society's "consensus," on everything from the consumer economy to gender roles, did not go unchallenged. Much discontent was channeled through the machine itself: advertisers sold rebellion no less than they sold baking soda. And yet others were rejecting the old ways, choosing new lifestyles, challenging old hierarchies, and embarking upon new paths.

[…]

Notes

16. Lewis L. Gould, *Watching Television Come of Age: The New York Times Reviews by Jack Gould* (Austin: University of Texas Press, 2002), 186.

17. Gary Edgerton, *Columbia History of American Television* (New York: Columbia University Press, 2009), 90.

18. Ibid., 178.

19. Christopher H. Sterling and John Michael Kittross, *Stay Tuned: A History of American Broadcasting* (New York: Routledge, 2001), 364.

20. Bruce Springsteen, "SXSW Keynote Address, *Rolling Stone* (March 28, 2012), http://www.rollingstone.com/music/news/exclusive-the-complete-text-of-bruce-springsteens-sxsw-keynote-address-20120328.

21. John D'Emilio, *Sexual Politics, Sexual Communities*, Second Edition (Chicago: University of Chicago Press, 2012), 102-103.

Mass Culture Still Marginalizes People of Color

Ruby Hamad

Ruby Hamad is an Australia-based writer who focuses on feminism and race. She's penned pieces for outlets like the Sydney Morning Herald, *the* Daily Life, *and the* Drum.

[…]

Race representation in popular culture may not be a blip on the radar of middle class white feminists—because it does not affect them—but for Women of Colour (WoC) who rarely see themselves reflected in magazines, it matters. A lot. Failing to consider this makes feminism dangerously irrelevant to many WoC. So much so, in fact, that many black women in the US have given up on the label altogether, preferring the term "womanist."

In the early '90s, Elizabeth Spelman published *Inessential Woman: Problems of Exclusion in Feminist Thought*, in which she argued that feminism was marginalising WoC due to its tendency to ignore how race, class and ethnicity react with sexism to affect non-white women.

Spelman wrote that for feminism to be inclusive, it had to acknowledge the unique experiences of WoC and allow them space to give their own accounts of their lives. She argued that feminism confuses "the condition of one group of women with the condition of all." In other words it is extremely marginalising for white feminists, who occupy a position of relative privilege, to lecture WoC on which issues should be important to them.

There seems to be a prevailing view that a step forward for one is a step for all. The furor over *Girls*, Lena Dunham's breakthrough TV show, demonstrates how WoC are expected to "take one for the

"When Racism Becomes a White Person's Issue," by Ruby Hamad, Fairfax Media, May 16, 2013. Reprinted by Permission.

team," even as they are excluded from the benefits of a supposed feminist victory.

Dunham's extraordinary success has been rightly hailed but, as criticism of the show's lack of characters from non-white, non-privileged backgrounds shows, it is a victory for some women only.

Although Dunham has tried to address this criticism, many white feminists seized on Dunham's words that she was simply writing about "people she knows." But would feminists accept this as a valid excuse from men who leave women out of films? Is it ever OK for privileged men to only "write what they know"?

Caitlin Moran, when asked if she planned to discuss *Girls*' lack of racial diversity in an interview with Dunham responded, "Nope. I literally couldn't give a shit about it."

Moran, one of feminism's major voices, and one which informed us *How to be a Woman*, literally couldn't give a shit about the ongoing exclusion of non-white women in the public space. Clearly, Moran is unfamiliar with the words of African-American feminist Barbara Smith: "Feminism is the political theory and practice that struggles to free all women: women of colour, working-class women, poor women, disabled women, Jewish women, lesbians, old women—as well as white, economically privileged heterosexual women. Anything less than this vision of total freedom is not feminism, but merely female self-aggrandisement."

As a woman of Arab-Muslim background I cannot divorce my experiences of being female from that of my race and religious background. While I am certainly pleased for Dunham at her success, I am also painfully aware that as a WoC—and a Muslim to boot—I cannot benefit in any meaningful way from it because it is a limited success that still actively excludes women like me.

As a writer I am fortunate to be given a public platform to express my views. Nonetheless, I find that whenever I write on issues of race and religion, I face such a strong backlash; it leaves me wondering if my work would attract the same hostility had a white woman penned it.

[…]

It seems to me there will always be a portion of the population that will regard me with suspicion. To them, I will always be the "other." In this I am reminded of the powerful words of black lesbian feminist Audre Lorde: "I cannot afford the luxury of fighting one form of oppression only. I cannot believe that freedom from intolerance is the right of only one particular group. And I cannot afford to choose between the front upon which I must battle these forces of discrimination, wherever they appear to destroy me. And when they appear to destroy me, it will not be long before they appear to destroy you."

And it is precisely this that leads me to write about issues such as race representation in fashion and the erasing of people of colour in film. Because it is this marginalisation that allows criticism of me based on nothing but my skin colour and my last name to flourish. Is it so surprising people don't trust Arabs given that, on those rare occasions when we do make it to the screen, it is overwhelmingly as terrorists or religious fanatics?

Without an understanding of how various forms of oppression intersect, feminism is meaningless. Success for some women is not a success for feminism because if feminism benefits only some women, some of the time, then that feminism is no feminism at all.

CHAPTER 3

Do National Tragedies Bring the Country Together?

Overview: Tragedy Unites, But Fear Divides

Stephanie A. Martin and Christopher Salinas

Stephanie A. Martin is an assistant professor of corporate communication and public affairs at Southern Methodist University. Christopher Salinas is a senior lecturer and director of public discourse at Southern Methodist University. They are both experts in political rhetoric.

Donald Trump's remarks in the aftermath of the Orlando shooting massacre—especially the reiteration of his call to temporarily ban Muslim immigration to the United States—angered leaders across America's political spectrum.

"This is not just a national security issue," Trump said. "It's a quality of life issue. If we want to protect the quality of life for all Americans—women and children, gay and straight, Jews and Christians and all people—then we need to tell the truth about radical Islam and we need to do it now."

Barack Obama called these words "dangerous" and against "democratic ideals." House Speaker Paul Ryan added that the "vast majority of Muslims in this country and around the world are moderate, they're peaceful, they're tolerant, and so they're among our best allies." And Hillary Clinton called Trump's ideas and approach "shameful."

As scholars of political rhetoric, we see parallels in Trump's speech to leaders and candidates who have tried to use fear to unite voters.

However, Trump takes the use of this rhetoric to a new level, using narrative devices that translate fear into anger, evoke doomsday scenarios and demonize entire groups of people.

"In the wake of tragedy, Trump takes rhetoric of fear to a whole new level," by Stephanie A. Martin and Christopher Salinas, The Conversation, June 15, 2016. https://theconversation.com/in-the-wake-of-tragedy-trump-takes-rhetoric-of-fear-to-a-whole-new-level-61069. Licensed Under CC BY-ND 4.0 International.

United against a shared threat

In the 1980s, a group of social psychologists developed Terror Management Theory, which is based on our (uniquely human) awareness that death is inevitable. According to the theory, people become anxious and scared when they're reminded of this fact. This fear, in turn, makes them more likely to coalesce around a shared identity or worldview: a religion, country, culture or ideology.

Of course, the vivid drama of terrorist attacks—people covered in blood, 911 calls, bodies piled up—are an especially effective means for reminding people of their own human frailty.

After attacks, politicians sometimes seek to capitalize on this vulnerability, turning speeches and press conferences into opportunities to rhetorically place the "nation" and cherished "freedoms" as at risk. The attack on a few becomes an attack on all. When speakers do this successfully, they are able to unite voters through a sense of shared threat.

In his address to the nation after the Pearl Harbor attacks, for example, Franklin Roosevelt declared that there would be "no blinking at the fact that our people, our territory and our interests [were] in grave danger."

His remarks that day, which became known as the "Infamy Speech," are generally regarded as having been crucial to Roosevelt's ability to both unite and reassure the public, while also marshaling widespread support for the country's formal entry into World War II.

George W. Bush used similar rhetoric on the night of September 11, 2001, when he said that the American "way of life [and] very freedom [had come] under attack in a series of deliberate and deadly terrorist acts."

Bush's approval ratings shot through the roof as political differences were cast aside in favor of national unity.

But, like almost all things Trump, the candidate's use of an already familiar rhetorical trope has been more sweeping than those that came before.

From fear to hate

Trump's discourse, both leading up to and following the Orlando shooting, begins with a pathos of fear but ends with an appeal to anger.

In rhetoric, pathos refers to arguments that appeal to the emotions of the audience, and appealing to emotion comes with inherent dangers. Yoda may have put it best in "Star Wars" when he warned, "Fear leads to anger. Anger leads to hate. Hate leads to suffering."

While Donald Trump may be no Jedi Master, his use of a pathos of fear suggests he is betting that he can turn the tail end of Yoda's warning—hate—into votes.

This requires, however, not so much the creation of fear— terrorism is real, and the Orlando shooting really happened— but, rather, finding ways to rhetorically stoke particular anxieties that already exist in the popular American consciousness: Crime. Unemployment. Lost freedom. Forgotten values.

Having raised these possibilities, Trump's next step is to present what amounts to a narrative of redemptive hate. Here, Trump offers to assuage the voter's fears through a mechanism of separation, as he erects a rhetorical wall between the desirable "us" and the undesirable "them."

Pick one or the other

Trump's speech given in response to the Orlando shootings reveals exactly how a political rhetoric of fear can create a dangerous rhetoric of division and anger.

Trump's rhetoric of fear begins with a framing device. He instructs his listeners to choose between two competing ideologies. They can continue to hold onto a "politically correct" worldview that makes it impossible to call a bad guy a bad guy, which, according to his (convoluted) logic, allows terror to happen. Or they can embrace his worldview, which will "straighten things out" and "make America great again."

Law professor Molly Wilson has pointed out how language that nudges listeners towards a particular option can be exceptionally persuasive, because it can cause individuals to change their minds far beyond their original preferences. In short, choices can be inspired—and limited—based on how they are presented.

If you ask your toddler whether he would prefer a turkey sandwich or tomato soup for lunch, you have framed his choices and limited his options. As adults, we know there are other choices he would probably prefer, like ice cream. But even there, you have set a misleading frame, because turkey sandwiches and tomato soup are hardly the only healthy choices for lunch, nor is ice cream the only unhealthy one that is available.

Politicians do the same thing in their rhetorical framing of issues, Trump markedly so. The way Trump presents it, you can either have political correctness and terror or insensitivity and freedom. To put it more bluntly, you can have Muslims and death or no Muslims and life. There are no other options.

A world on fire, a foe shared by all

Having set out this black and white worldview, Trump raises the stakes again by using apocalyptic language.

Just minutes into his June 13 speech about the Orlando attack, he aroused the possibility that—unless he's elected president—the United States might cease to exist.

"If we don't get tough and if we don't get smart, and fast, we're not going to have our country anymore," he said. "There will be nothing, absolutely nothing, left."

In addition to framing, rhetoricians refer to premises like the one Trump makes here as argumentum in terrorem, which is a form of logical fallacy stipulating that the failure to accept a premise will result in irreparable harm.

Studies have shown how when people are afraid, they tend to overestimate the probability that the thing feared will really happen. Wilson, the political framing expert, also notes that people are irrationally intolerant of risk when there is a potential for catastrophe. And Trump's rhetoric is rife with catastrophic possibility.

Finally, while Trump establishes fear through his apocalyptic words, he transforms that fear into actionable anger by creating a common enemy. In the Orlando speech, the common enemy is the Muslim. At other times in the campaign, Trump has demonized Latinos to similar effect.

The famed rhetorical theorist Kenneth Burke once critiqued Adolf Hitler's tome "Mein Kampf." There, Burke observed that "men (sic) who unite on nothing else can unite on the basis of a foe shared by all."

For Trump, the enemy is the Muslim, whether he's a terrorist or not.

"The Muslims have to work with us… They know what's going on. They know that [the Orlando shooter] was bad. They knew the people in San Bernardino were bad. But you know what? They didn't turn them in," he said the day after the Orlando shooting.

This is the rhetorical creation of a nameless, faceless enemy to fear. The gunman from Orlando has faded from view. Indeed, Trump goes so far as to say he'll "never say his name," leaving the listener to connect the dots and oppose anyone who might be like him in the least.

And so the circle is complete. Fear becomes anger. Anger becomes hate.

Whether Big or Small, Tragedies Trigger Powerful Fellow-Feeling

Ariel Gros-Werter

Ariel Gros-Werter's writing has appeared in the Huffington Post. *She holds an MBA from Vanderbilt University.*

When I worked in synagogues, I was amazed that regardless of pressing assignments, we dropped everything when a community member or congregant's relative died. All other responsibilities faded as we rushed to address the needs of the mourners. Messages were drafted and triple-checked for wording and name spellings before emailing the community about the death, the funeral and burial details, and where and when the mourners would welcome friends offering comfort and condolences. Food packages and school pick-ups were arranged so the family would not need to think about these mundane details. Indeed, the community quickly came together in multiple ways to support the family and mourn their loss with them. I was so impressed by our unexpected expediency and level of care that I joked "we did death well."

I rarely had personal connections with the deceased who were nearly always older and died from natural or medical causes. As a young professional living in a safe neighborhood, death to me was the realm of unknown others or those in my parents' or grandparents' generation. I never expected to be faced with a sudden unnatural death of one of my peers while in my 20s. But then the reports came out that Taylor Force, a fellow student at the Owen Graduate School of Management in the MBA class below mine, died from a terrorist stabbing on Tuesday while on a student trip to Israel.

I didn't know Taylor well, yet I am part of the community coming together in the face of this tragedy. Community. We saw

"Tragedy Brings Us Together," by Ariel Gros-Werter, TheHuffingtonPost.com, Inc., March 15, 2017. Reprinted by Permission.

it materialize in the wake of 9/11 when America unified to mourn and we New Yorkers reached out to care for each other. We saw it after Hurricanes Katrina and Sandy as Americans came together to help rebuild. We've seen it in the aftermath of every school shooting. Tragedy causes us to come together.

This tragedy also amplifies our sense of community at Owen. Emails were sent to the entire university, colleagues posted on our class Facebook group asking what we could do, our Dean kept us updated about the other students on the trip and upcoming memorials, a classmate relayed info about a campaign to raise money to support Taylor's family, people began replying "going" to a memorial to be held this week at school, coffee in the school lobby to bring students together, an email informed us his sister asks that donations in his name be sent to the Wounded Warrior Project®.

While I did not know Taylor well, I had seen him in the hallways at school and met him a few times over the last 7 months; he was more than just a name and a story. I was amazed, therefore, when speaking to an Owen alumna who had never met Taylor, she asked to be kept informed because she and other alumni from the class of 2014 wanted to make donations in his honor.

The heightened sense of community following this tragedy is far-reaching. It not only spans the Owen community and Taylor's personal and professional networks, but much of the country. This has circulated through media and social media channels because it touches all of us. We connect with Taylor and are in shock at what happened. Taylor was a fellow American, on vacation, a husband, a friend, a colleague. Like many of us he wanted to be more. He was a West Point graduate, a veteran who served our country in Iraq and Afghanistan, and was pursuing higher education.

After a tragedy, everything is seen through a larger perspective and in this wider view our personal woes lose their immediacy. We put aside our differences and come together in our sadness. Tragedies make us recognize how precious our friends and family are. Petty disagreements fall away as we realize how random tragedy can be—Taylor was in the wrong place at the wrong time—how easily he could have been elsewhere or it could have been someone else. The outpouring of support for Taylor's family is moving and completely appropriate.

We should not need a tragedy to come together. On an ongoing basis, we need to shed our differences, to reach out and build our communities, to always make sure people know how important they are to us.

Social Media Is an Outlet for Empathy, But It Can Be an Echo Chamber

Doug Bernard

Doug Bernard writes about cyber-issues for the Voice of America. He has also written for the New York Times, *the* Christian Science Monitor, SPIN *and NPR.*

For more than a decade, millions of people turned to social networking and media sites such as Twitter and Facebook to learn the latest news.

The massacre on Sunday at the Orlando nightclub Pulse was no different. For example, a Snapchat video by clubgoer Amanda Alvear that accidentally captured the first moments of gunfire inside the club quickly went viral, even before major news outlets began reporting on the attack.

Increasingly, especially in times of tragedy and trauma, social researchers say people turn to their online communities for news, for solace, to share painful experiences of confusion and sadness, and reach out to friends for emotional support and counsel.

Nothing about the Internet is purely good or bad, and those same social networks that can help bring people together can also often be used to drive them apart. In this instance, it took almost no time for acrimonious fights to start over placing the blame, the threats of Islamist terrorism, gun control, presidential politics and LGBT rights.

So, is social media a help or a hindrance in times of crisis and tragedy? The answer, perhaps unsurprisingly, is both.

"Social Media Unites, Divides in Times of Tragedy," by Doug Bernard, VOA News, June 13, 2016, https://www.voanews.com/a/social-media-orlando-shooting/3374048.html.

Sharing and oversharing

"With social media, we can now connect with millions of people, including strangers, remotely," says Tomas Chamorro-Premuzi, a business psychology professor at University College London and Columbia University. "Such a connection is mostly digital, but human imagination enables us to experience empathy, what other people feel, even when they are far away and we don't know them."

Chamorro-Premuzic says that social networks can function something like watching a sad movie: collectively, individuals can share their emotional responses together as part of a community. When overused, it can reduce profound, complex emotions and issues into talking points and babble.

"The perpetual need to overshare opinions and feelings does trivialize the expression of emotions over social media. It is not the same to lose a close friend than to change the profile picture of your Facebook page," he told VOA.

"Social media is an amplified, yet more superficial, version of spending physical time with a close friend. Fundamentally, our emotions haven't changed, but social media is used to broadcast them more widely. It is harder to suffer in private now. Everybody thinks they ought to share," said Chamorro-Premuzic.

Another issue researchers are studying is how social media can rapidly drive individuals to their "safe spot," the place they're most comfortable personally and ideologically, and close off opinions that are different from their core values and beliefs.

This, says Charles Steinfeld, is especially true at moments of pain and confusion, such as with the Orlando massacre.

"Social media conversations tend to connect like-minded people, so it isn't as likely to bridge big ideological divides and is more likely to deepen divisions," says Steinfeld, a professor in the Department of Media and Information at Michigan State University.

But Steinfeld says that tendency is not a hard and fast rule.

"In many cases, our connections on social media may have arisen because of similarities in one area of our lives. For example, we work in the same company, but our views on other topics are different. So we do at times see people in our network of connections making statements that are inconsistent with our own views."

Reinforcing belief and bias

One main problem with social media use during crises, said Tomas Chamorro-Premuzic, it that it enhances "confirmation bias," or the tendency to seek out and listen to only that information that reinforces long-standing opinions.

"We mostly pay attention to those who think like we do," he said. "It was no surprise to see that Facebook edits the news feed to promote liberal news, for most of its users are probably liberal.

Likewise, we like and share comments and content from those who share our views, which perpetuates a vicious cycle and makes people more narrow-minded."

"On social media it is more tempting to believe that our views are the truth, because we are only exposed to opposite views in small doses."

And, says Steinfeld, confirmation bias affects not just the sources we seek out for news and information, but those we're most likely to listen to and share.

"It's just more common that the people in our network tend to agree with us on the big issues—like gun control, abortion rights, immigration, and so on. So the discourse on these topics is more likely to be pretty one-sided within a person's social network," he cautions.

Just hours after news began to circulate of the murder of 49 people at a gay nightclub in Orlando, millions of flame-filled arguments and accusations filled social networks of all sorts, all the while millions of others posted messages of condolence, support and love for all those touched by the shootings.

For those hurt or "unfriended" on social media in the wake of the tragedy, Tomas Chamorro-Premuzic says the best thing to do is put yourself first.

"There is no etiquette here if you are really hurt," he said. "Do what makes you feel better. Mourning and grief are normal human emotions and they won't get better or worse because of social media."

The Tragedy of the Orlando Massacre Spurred Partisan Rancor

Margaret Wente

Margaret Wente is a longtime columnist for the Globe and Mail, *Canada's largest paper, and a board member of the Energy Probe Research Foundation.*

Today, 9/11 seems as if it happened in another century. After the planes hit the towers, Americans stood united in their grief and solidarity. They cast aside their partisanship to mourn the dead.

Orlando was different. The bodies were scarcely cold by the time the shouting began. On the Sunday talk shows, people sounded as if they were talking about two entirely different events. "ISIS VS. US" blared the headline in the *New York Post* on Monday, invoking the spectre of a global jihad. The *Daily News* blamed guns. "Thanks, NRA," it shrilled.

In the immediate aftermath, Donald Trump blamed radical Islam but refused to mention the word "guns." Barack Obama blamed guns and terror but couldn't bring himself to mention the words radical Islam.

The Orlando massacre is undoubtedly a windfall for the Trump campaign. He's thumping his chest for looking prescient. It will fire up his anti-Muslim blather and harden his support. It also poses a major test for Mr. Obama, Hillary Clinton and the Democrats. If they can't bring themselves to say that radical Islamist ideology is a challenge to Western values and national security, their credibility will be in tatters.

Meantime, plenty of people argued that the real culprit was homophobia and intolerance – not just the shooter's, but ours. As

"How Orlando Divides America," by Margaret Wente, The Globe and Mail Inc., June 15, 2016. Reprinted by Permission.

Mr. Obama put it, "we need the strength and courage to change" our attitudes toward the gay, lesbian, bisexual and transgender community. Funny, but I was under the impression that most of Western society had already done that. Nonetheless, a lot of gays and liberals took the opportunity to go on anti-Republican rants, arguing that the philosophy of jihadism and the philosophy of gun-toting U.S. religious conservatives aren't so different.

Actually, one difference occurs to me. No U.S. conservative legislators advocate the death penalty for homosexuality. Nor do they celebrate when more than a hundred gay people are mowed down by a terrorist at a night club.

"The only shock was that it took this long for some jihadist to go after a gay establishment," wrote Bruce Bawer at *City Journal*. Mr. Bawer, who is gay, has spent years warning about the soft-pedalling of Islamist extremism. He believes that certain Muslim values are fundamentally incompatible with Western tolerance and liberalism. For example, most of the world's 1.5 billion Muslims belong to cultures that believe homosexuality is morally wrong.

The shooter claimed he was inspired by Islamic State, which believes that homosexuals should be flung from tall buildings. According to his father, shortly before the massacre he was enraged by the sight of two men kissing. The father also denied that the massacre had anything to do with religion, which seems a touch disingenuous.

Homophobic attitudes are also found among Western Muslims. According to a recent survey, more than half of British Muslims (52 per cent) think homosexuality should be illegal. Nearly half (47 per cent) think gay people shouldn't be allowed to teach in schools.

Does this mean we should ban Muslim immigration? No. What it means is that we need to be alert to the challenges of integration. The vast majority of Muslims are peaceful, law-abiding folks. The truth is that both homophobia and Islamophobia are deeply wrong. But in a polarized society, these more complicated truths are likely to get lost.

It's the same with gun control. As one commenter wrote, there's "a simple answer to these questions: get assault weapons off the street." If only he were right. Of course assault weapons should be banned. But that alone won't stop terrorist attacks. The Boston Marathon attackers used nail bombs. The Paris shooters wiped out 130 people with weapons they obtained in a country that has strict gun control. Dangerous extremists will always find a way, especially in open societies that frown on preventive detention and value freedom of speech.

From what we know so far, Omar Mateen seemed like a typical lone wolf: an angry, self-radicalized Muslim who wasn't particularly religious until he was infected by the virus of extremist ideology. Maybe the FBI, who had him on its radar, should have tailed him more closely. But there are probably hundreds of potential Omar Mateens around, and it's impossible to tell which ones will blow. Constant surveillance isn't possible and rounding them up in advance isn't legal. Raining bombs on the enemy abroad (as Mr. Trump seems to want to do) is no solution either.

For all the blood and treasure shed since 9/11, we seem no closer to figuring out how to stop terrorist attacks against the West—and in some ways we seem farther away than ever. The other difference between then and now is that Americans can't even discuss the problem without yelling past each other.

After Orlando, White Nationalists Unleashed a Wave of Violent Rhetoric

Eyes on the Right

Eyes on the Right is the internet handle of a blogger at Angrywhitemen .org, a site that tracks the new white nationalist movement.

Following the deadly attack on a gay nightclub in Orlando that left 49 dead and many others seriously wounded, cheers erupted on alt-right websites like the Daily Stormer. Not only was this an attack on the LGBT community—a group reviled by many white nationalists—but the shooter, Omar Mateen, was a Muslim man of Afghan descent.

In the days following the deadliest shooting by a single perpetrator in American history, the hashtag #ShootBack became a rallying cry for Islamophobes, most of whom never lifted a finger to support gay rights in the past. Elsewhere, white nationalists decided to exploit the tragedy to push for a ban on Muslim immigrants.

Over at the Right Stuff, the website that gave birth to the anti-Semitic echo meme, an article by Butch Leghorn advocated using the shooting to fracture the left's "coalition." As Leghorn wrote, "The Democrats are pro-Islam and, objectively, to be pro-Islam is to be anti-Gay." Therefore, the bloodbath in Orlando serves as a "very valuable wedge issue." The alt-right, he said, must "hammer this issue."

"Meme magic is real boys, so spread this meme. Drive this wedge. Smash their coalition. Make it cool to be anti-Muslim because Liberalism."

Since the shooting can be used to justify a ban on Muslim immigrants or a mass expulsion of Muslims from American soil, Leghorn advocated that the alt-right "exploit this sentiment," and

"White Nationalists Exploit Orlando Tragedy to Drive a Wedge Between Muslims and the LGBT Community," by Eyes on the Right, Angrywhitemen.org, https://angrywhitemen. org/2016/07/30/white-nationalists-exploit-orlando-tragedy-to-drive-a-wedge-between-muslims-and-the-lgbt-community/. July 30, 2016. Reprinted by Permission.

drive "this wedge as deeply as possible to break off the pro-Gay coalition into the Trump camp." He suggested using images of a rainbow flag with phrases such as "F**k Islam" and "Trump."

Exactly who would be suckered by such an obvious ploy is beyond me, but that didn't stop alt-right figurehead Milo Yiannopoulos from attempting to rally the LGBT community to the anti-Muslim, pro-gun side. At a June 15, 2016 speech in Orlando, Yiannopoulos declared:

Gay people need an end to gun free zones. Gay people need and end to the pointless pacifism of the left because we have a threat on our shores, in our communities, in our societies, in streets not far from here, that requires a response from the minorities the left has given up on. It refuses to protect us, instead it pits us against each other. It creates a victimhood hierarchy with Muslims at the top, well the problem with putting Muslims at the top is they want to kill everyone else on the list.

A month later, during the RNC, the conservative troll held a "Gays for Trump" party, which saw guests the likes of Pamela Geller and Geert Wilders—both well known anti-Muslim activists. Prior to this, however, Yiannopoulos has never been particularly friendly to the LGBT community. He is fond of mocking transgender people, said straight people should be able to use anti-gay slurs, and admitted that he wishes he were born straight. It would be foolish to interpret these stunts as anything other than an excuse to bash the American Muslim community.

On the July 12, 2016 episode of *Radio 3Fourteen* (a popular white supremacist podcast hosted by Lana Lokteff), SeventhSon and Mike Enoch—two co-hosts of the Right Stuff's *Daily Shoah*— discussed the adoption of the echo meme by Jews, and the implications of the Orlando massacre. Jews "definitely thought they were taking some term back" by using the echoes, said SeventhSon, which is "ridiculous because all you're doing is helping us now." The point of the echo meme, he said, was to identify journalists and others who advocate "positions that are anti-white, that are anti-American," and help people make the connection to their Jewish heritage.

SeventhSon added that taking the echoes back isn't the same as "the N-word that, you know, the rappers can start using it and it becomes cool." Mike Enoch wondered whether Jews and their allies were "expecting to have the same success that blacks had when they took back the word 'nigger,'" and joked that since African-Americans reclaimed the N-word "it's been a smashing success for blacks, I mean, *look at the accomplishments they've had* since they did that."

Later on in the episode Lokteff brought up the Orlando shooting, or "Allah gay bar" as she derisively put it. "Whether they blame, they blame Islam, people blame Zionists, false fags [sic], you know, they want muh guns, you got immigration, you've got multiculturalism," she said. "I mean really, to me, the problem is just *Leftists*. They use all these things against white people to destroy our civilization, right? It's like an amalgamation of degenerate forces, what do you guys think?"

Mike Enoch called the tragedy a "narrative smorgasbord for us" that "doesn't stop giving" because it pits "one Leftist client group" against another. The Left is nothing but an "anti-white coalition" made up of "marginalized" groups that are used "as a club" against white people. "The wedge that we've been trying to drive—and I've done this, people might've seen me doing this on Facebook and elsewhere—you drive that wedge, you say…'Look, pro-Islam is anti-gay,'" he advised.

"Push that slogan and you'll see, you see they don't know what the f**k to do with it because, again, you see people, you see that the people who are interested in maintaining the Leftist coalition and the Leftist consensus of every non-white, non-traditional identity against white people, people that are really interested in that, and that's, like, ideological Leftists—be they Jews or just, like, you know, elites—that wanna maintain that, and that that's what they're more interested in."

America's Pernicious Racial Divisions

John W. Whitehead

John W. Whitehead is an attorney focused on constitutional law and human rights. In 1982, he founded the civil liberties organization the Rutherford Institute.

> *"How can you thank a man for giving you what's already yours? How then can you thank him for giving you only part of what's already yours? You haven't even made progress, if what's being given to you, you should have had already. That's no progress."*
>
> —Malcolm X, 1964

In 1964, the United States was in the throes of racial conflict. Civil rights activists were leading black Americans and their white allies in a struggle against institutionalized racism, segregation, and disenfranchisement. The situation was bleak, activists were being murdered, the government seemed deadlocked on the issue, and many were losing hope. However, the passage of the Civil Rights Act and the Voting Rights Act set the stage for a positive transformation in race relations in a country that had been plagued by racial tension since its inception.

We have yet to live up to that hoped-for transformation. Almost 50 years later, despite having made demonstrable progress on the race issue, the idea that we live in a "post-racial" society is simply a myth—a myth that was given a boost last week when the

"The Myth of a Post-Racial America," by John W. Whitehead, The Rutherford Institute, July 1, 2013. Reprinted by Permission.

U.S. Supreme Court invalidated Section 4 of the Voting Rights Act, legislation enacted during the Civil Rights Era which was critical to the enfranchisement of black Americans living in the Jim Crow South. Writing for the majority, Chief Justice Roberts claimed that times had changed since the 1960s, and the section of the law requiring historically racist sections of the country to have changes to their elections laws vetted by the federal government was anachronistic.

Superficially, Roberts' claims ring true. Obviously Americans have made great strides in confronting issues of race since the 1960s. *De jure* segregation has been eliminated, minority groups have greater access to essential goods and services, and we have seen what many thought would never happen, the election of a black man to the office of the presidency.

Yet looking past the veil of progress which clouds the vision of well-meaning people who believe the issue of racism has been solved, we can easily see that there are many policies and practices in America which perpetuate the inequality of races. The following is a brief rundown of the many fronts on which America continues to fail to live up to its "post-racial" ideal.

The criminal justice system.

The starkest example of racial discrimination in America today is the treatment of blacks and other minorities in the criminal justice system. The statistics are astounding. Consider that:

- There are more blacks in the corrections system today— whether in prison or on probation or parole—than were enslaved in 1850.
- People of color account for 30% of the total population in America, yet comprise 60% of the prison population.
- Blacks that commit federal crimes on average receive sentences that are ten percent longer than their white counterparts.
- One in three black men will see the inside of a prison in his lifetime.
- Blacks and Hispanics are much more likely to face interaction with police officers, are three times as likely to be searched

during a traffic stop, and four times as likely to be the target of the use of police force.

War on drugs.

A good deal of the disproportionate impact of the corrections system on blacks and other minorities is due to the government's relentless, fruitless pursuit known as the Drug War. Consider that:

- Only 14 percent of drug users are black, but blacks constitute 37 percent of those arrested for drug crimes.
- Blacks make up 50% of state and local inmates imprisoned for drug crimes.
- Black youth are ten times as likely as their white counterparts to be arrested for drug crimes, despite the fact that whites are more likely to abuse drugs.

Then you have the proliferation of SWAT team raids used to enforce drug laws and execute search warrants, sometimes resulting in the deaths of innocent people like Jose Guerena and Aiyana Jones—both of whom were "brown skinned."

Stop and frisk.

The New York Police Department's infamous stop and frisk policy, which involves beat cops targeting citizens going about their daily business for pat downs and interrogations, is primarily directed toward black and Latino citizens. The number of stop and frisks occurring on the streets of New York has exploded in the past ten years, jumping from 97,000 in 2002 to nearly 686,000 in 2011. Of all of those stops, only two percent result in uncovering an illegal weapon.

Of all the stop and frisks occurring in 2012, over 86 percent involved African-Americans or Latinos. Even in precincts with the lowest percentage of minority residents, blacks and Latinos still made up more than 70 percent of all stops. Despite targeting minorities, a stop conducted against a white person was more likely to uncover an illegal weapon or contraband than stopping a black or Latino person.

Education.

Even in the realm of education, one of the first battlegrounds where civil rights activists were victorious, segregation and inequality continue to rear their heads in the 21st century. Indeed, as judicial oversight of school systems has waned in the years since *Brown v. Board of Education*, schools have become increasingly segregated.

Some researchers have suggested that American public schools are more segregated now than they were in the 1960s. A report released in September 2012 by the Civil Rights Project at UCLA reported a number of troubling trends and statistics, including the fact that "fifteen percent of black students and 14 percent of Latino students attend 'apartheid schools' across the nation in which whites make up zero to 1 percent of the enrollment."

In addition to being segregated, students of color are much more likely to be punished, and punished more severely than their white peers. During the 2009-10 school year, 96,000 students were arrested and 242,000 referred to law enforcement officials. Of those students, more than 70 percent were black or Hispanic.

The right to vote.

To bring it back to where we started, the Supreme Court's assertion that the issue of universal suffrage has been solved, even in the most historically racist sections of the country, is simply false.

Due to felon disenfranchisement, one in thirteen African-Americans cannot vote. In some states, such as Virginia, that number rises to one in five. As of 2004, more black men were disenfranchised than in 1870, the year the Fifteenth Amendment, which bars racial discrimination at the voting booth, was ratified.

In the wake of the Supreme Court's decision in *Shelby County v. Holder*, these disparities will only get worse. While the Voter ID laws which states attempted to implement prior to the 2012 elections were largely blocked due to federal oversight and judicial appeals, the Supreme Court has just done away with any major impediment to these attempts to purge legitimate voters from the rolls in a disingenuous attempt to protect the integrity of elections.

Indeed, attempting to purge voter rolls based upon specious accusations of voter fraud is now the predominant method of discouraging or preventing minorities from voting. Reducing the number of polling places and cutting polling place hours is another tried and true method, and we will only see more attempts as the results of the Supreme Court's decision play out.

Arguing for Shelby County before the U.S. Supreme Court, attorney Bert Rein referred to racism as an "old disease" and claimed that "that disease is cured. That problem is solved." What has been solved is not the issue of racism, but a public relations issue. Racism is still alive and well in America; it has simply taken on a more insidious character, and doesn't feature the bigoted rants of the Dixiecrats of old. Instead it manifests itself in the public schools, the criminal justice system, the electoral process, and elsewhere, under the veil of seemingly colorblind policies which still tend to target those who have been historically disadvantaged in this country.

As Michelle Alexander explains in her book *The New Jim Crow: Mass Incarceration in the Age of Colorblindness*, which explains how America's so-called War on Drugs has been a vehicle for reinstituting some of the most egregious policies of the Jim Crow era, we may have changed the face of America, but underneath we still operate much the same as we always have.

> What has changed since the collapse of Jim Crow has less to do with the basic structure of our society than with the language we use to justify it. In the era of colorblindness, it is no longer socially permissible to use race, explicitly, as a justification for discrimination, exclusion, and social contempt.
>
> So we don't. Rather than rely on race, we use our criminal justice system to label people of color 'criminals' and then engage in all the practices we supposedly left behind. Today it is perfectly legal to discriminate against criminals in nearly all the ways that it was once legal to discriminate against African Americans. Once you're labeled a felon, the old forms of discrimination— employment discrimination, housing discrimination, denial of the right to vote, denial of educational opportunity, denial of

food stamps and other public benefits, and exclusion from jury service—are suddenly legal. As a criminal, you have scarcely more rights, and arguably less respect, than a black man living in Alabama at the height of Jim Crow. We have not ended racial caste in America; we have merely redesigned it.

CHAPTER 4

Did the 2016 Presidential Election Divide America Beyond Repair?

Overview: The US Election: Racism and Sexism, Pessimism and Division

Nick O'Malley

Nick O'Malley is a senior writer and the former United States correspondent for the Sydney Morning Herald *and the* Age.

I n 2004 a little known senator from Illinois gave the keynote address at the Democratic Party convention.

He voiced his belief that America was stronger, and more itself, when unified.

"It is that fundamental belief—I am my brother's keeper, I am my sister's keeper—that makes this country work," he said. "It's what allows us to pursue our individual dreams, and yet still come together as one American family. *E pluribus unum.* Out of many, one."

"Even as we speak, there are those who are preparing to divide us, the spin masters, the negative ad peddlers who embrace the politics of anything goes.

"Well, I say to them tonight, there is not a liberal America and a conservative America; there is the United States of America. There is not a black America and white America and Latino America and Asian America; there is the United States of America."

When Barack Obama left the stage in Boston that night the stadium exploded. Moments later the MSNBC host Chris Matthews said on air: "I have seen the first black president."

Four years later Obama became the president, and his message of unity never faltered. He voiced it again on Monday night in Pennsylvania at a rally for Hillary Clinton, and again on Wednesday in the White House rose garden surrounded by sobbing staff as he addressed the nation and called for an orderly transfer of power to the administration of the 45th president, Donald Trump.

"US election: Divided America," by Nick O'Malley, the Sydney Morning Herald, November 11, 2016. Reprinted by Permission.

Whether he believed it to be a truth or an ideal is not clear.

But on Tuesday night the nation he has led for the past eight years offered its own verdict, voting along lines marked by race and class.

Exit polls showed that for the first time white Americans voted almost as a bloc, in much the way minority groups have historically. Trump won the white vote 58 per cent to 37 per cent.

More significantly he won the white working class vote that once supported the Democrats. This is how Clinton lost the so-called "blue firewall" of states, such as Wisconsin and Michigan, where she had barely bothered campaigning.

Clinton won 65 per cent of the Latino vote. But what perhaps cost Clinton the White House was the absence of the expected surge of Latino voters.

Hispanics made up 11 per cent of the electorate, only one percentage point more than during the last election. And in the end Trump outperformed Mitt Romney among Latino voters, 29 to 27 per cent. Given Clinton's huge outreach effort and Trump's promises of walls and deportation this is a shocking result.

Clinton won 88 per cent of the black vote. This looks overwhelming but it was not a good number for her. Obama, unsurprisingly had won far more, with 95 per cent, but Clinton's campaign had hoped more would turn out for her.

She was also hurt by a reduction in turnout, which fell among African Americans from 13 per cent of the electorate to 12 per cent.

Obama will have noticed this slump. In early November he told African Americans in a speech he would take it as a "personal insult" if they did not vote for Clinton.

"My name may not be on the ballot, but our progress is on the ballot," he said at a Congressional Black Caucus Foundation gala dinner in Washington. "Tolerance is on the ballot. Democracy is on the ballot. Justice is on the ballot."

The electorate was also divided by its level of education. In 2012 Obama won the votes of people with college degrees and those without. Four years later Clinton won voters with a college degree, 52 per cent to 43 per cent, while Trump won voters without a college degree by 8 per cent.

Another surprise of the result was the role women played.

Ninety-four per cent of African American women and 68 per cent of Hispanic women voted for Clinton. The latter was not as high a percentage as the Democrat probably hoped for, but it was a decisive majority nonetheless. There was just one problem: white women.

Fifty-three per cent of white women voted for Trump, a man who has been accused of sexual assault by more than ten women. Breaking the numbers into smaller chunks, we find that a bare majority of college-educated white women, 51 per cent, voted for Clinton, while 62 per cent of women with less than a college education supported Trump. White women, then, comprised a critical part of Trump's winning bloc.

It wasn't supposed to be this way. Clinton often wore "suffragette white" to signify the historic nature of her candidacy. On election day, hundreds flocked to the Rochester, New York grave site of Susan B. Anthony, the pioneering leader of the American suffrage movement. Many women placed "I voted" stickers on the tombstone as a tribute to the woman who was arrested in 1872 for voting. Anthony died in 1906, 14 years before the right of all women to vote was codified in the 19th Amendment—often called the Susan B. Anthony amendment—of the US constitution.

The exit polls tell us a few things. It reflects a nation even more bitterly divided than it was on that day Obama introduced himself to history with that speech in Boston. The divisions in this nation between white and other minorities, between rich and poor, between rural and urban, are wider now than on the day he entered office.

The Pew Research Centre published data on Thursday that revealed the depth of these divisions. These groups not only do not see eye to eye on key issues, they disagree on what issues are key.

Nearly 80 per cent of Trump voters said illegal immigration was a "very big" problem in the country, while just 20 per cent of Clinton voters said the same.

Nearly three quarters of Trump supporters (74 per cent) believed terrorism was a very big problem, compared with 42 per cent of Clinton supporters.

Crime and jobs, including job opportunities for working-class Americans, also were rated as more serious problems by Trump voters than Clinton voters.

Clinton voters cared about climate change (66 per cent cited it as a very big problem), while Trump voters did not (14 per cent).

Clinton backers also believed gun violence and the gap between rich and poor were much more serious problems.

Both racism and sexism were viewed as more serious problems among Clinton voters than Trump voters.

Unsurprisingly, Trump voters took a uniformly negative view of progress over the past eight years.

Indeed the only thing that both groups of voters agreed on was how dimly they viewed both candidates. Sixty one per cent of people who were interviewed shortly before polling day said if Trump were elected, he would definitely or probably not set a high moral standard for the presidency; and 57 per cent said he would not improve America's global standing.

Half of the people said he would probably use his presidency to enrich himself or his friends. Two thirds of voters believed Clinton would not lead an open and transparent government if she were elected.

By the most elemental measures Pew found Trump and Clinton voters were marked by their differences. Just on 60 per cent of Trump supporters said "honour and duty" were their core values, compared with 35 per cent of Clinton's voters. Clinton's voters valued "compassion and helping others."

The fact America is divided is not news, and the increase in that division since Obama's election will surely go down as one of his keen regrets.

But it is also causing tension within both the parties. The Republican Party, flushed with victory, is at the moment presenting a unified face. But its establishment was horrified by the way Trump conducted a campaign designed to attract white voters by exciting racial anxieties.

Its chairman, Reince Priebus, is now being considered as Trump's chief of staff. After the Republican Party's 2012 campaign he endorsed an internal party study known as the "the autopsy," calling on the party to reach out to minority groups.

The autopsy declared demographic changes dictated that the party could no longer reach out to white voters and expect to win. Trump ignored the experts and gambled he could squeeze one more victory out of the strategy.

In the Democratic Party many people are furious Clinton, and to an extent Obama before her, gave up on the white working-class vote that once made up the party's base, to target a coalition of minority voters that have been driven from the Republican Party.

"The Democratic Party once represented the working class," Robert Reich, an economist who once served as Bill Clinton's labor secretary, wrote this week.

"But over the last three decades the party has been taken over by Washington-based fundraisers, bundlers, analysts, and pollsters who have focused instead on raising campaign money from corporate and Wall Street executives, and getting votes from upper middle-class households in 'swing' suburbs."

In a divided and pessimistic nation, the Democratic Party has begun its own autopsy.

In a Distrustful Nation, Divisions Are Hard to Repair

Mary Kay Magistad

Mary Kay Magistad is a journalist for Public Radio International. She has worked as the World's *East Asia correspondent and also written for NPR, the* Washington Post, *and the* Boston Globe.

Trust is what lets you enter into relationships with friends, lovers and business partners. It's what lets you walk down the street and go to farmers markets, concerts and sporting events, knowing that you'll be safe among strangers. You'll be fine.

Trust is also part of what lets a democracy function. Trust in democratic institutions, formal and informal—the integrity of the vote, the balance of power, the role of serious journalism, the idea that—while politics can be a dirty business, most people play fair, most of the time.

That includes accepting when the other side wins, and respecting the rules of the game. It includes not calling into question the integrity of the very system in which you serve.

But the man who is about to become president spent years claiming his predecessor wasn't an American citizen—when he is, and always has been. Candidate Donald Trump said repeatedly that the system is rigged, and that he might not accept the election results unless he won. He insinuated that his supporters should think about taking out the other candidate, if she won. Since being elected, he has questioned the competence and integrity of the US intelligence community. He has nominated heads of government departments who are on record saying they'd like to gut or get rid of those very departments.

And he has regularly denigrated journalists—real journalists— while staying apparently sanguine about the fake news that his

"America Is Divided—And That's by Design," by Mary Kay Magistad, Public Radio International, January 12, 2017. Reprinted by Permission.

supporters shared around during the campaign, to help gain support. Ironically, purveyors of fake news loved Donald Trump, because his supporters were willing to believe just about anything that made him look good, and his opponents look bad. When unverified documents were released, suggesting that the Russians have dirt on him, he called it disgraceful fake news, and releasing it was like what Nazi Germany used to do.

He appears to be much more concerned about the making public of those documents, than of the US intelligence community's unanimous finding that Russian leader Vladimir Putin ordered and oversaw a covert campaign to throw the US election to Trump.

So what's a citizen to believe, or to trust?

"This is a time of testing of our democratic system" says Thomas Mann, a senior fellow at the Brookings Institution, a scholar who for half a century has studied and written about American governance. "This is the first real threat we've had in a long time, and will the institutions and rules and norms be sufficient to keep us from falling the way of many other countries toward a more authoritarian leadership."

Mann is co-author with Norman Ornstein, of the American Enterprise Institute, of the books "The Broken Branch: How Congress Is Failing America" (2006) and "It's Even Worse Than It Looks: How the American Constitutional System Collided With the New Politics of Extremism." The second book, released in 2012, struck a chord, went viral, and was even read in part on the floor of the US Senate. Its rerelease in 2016 has the word "looks" crossed out in the title. It now reads: "It's Even Worse Than It Was."

"Perhaps the most worrisome is the absence of acceptance of facts and truth—even science," Mann says. "It's the dispute among elites and with ordinary citizens about what should be taken as the basis of beginning a conversation. Donald Trump has set new records in espousing all kind of thoughts that are patently untrue. And it doesn't bother him one bit and he may or may not know it is when he's making those statements. It's kind of Orwellian."

But the rot didn't start with Trump, Mann and Ornstein argue in their books. Rather, they say, it started as a deliberate strategy by some Republicans almost four decades ago, to pry away from the Democratic Party the lock on Congress they'd enjoyed for the four decades up to that point. Mann says he and Ornstein first encountered the idea for the strategy when interviewing a newly elected House representative after the 1978 midterm election—Newt Gingrich.

"Newt outlined a strategy to achieve that objective by basically destroying the legitimacy of Congress as an institution and the people who occupy it, and lowering public trust in government," Mann says. "He thought the only way to throw off the majority Democrats was to discredit the institution and their leadership of it. And he worked hard at it and created the Conservative Opportunity Society, some of which was substantive and ideological. But mainly he was out there recruiting and training candidates in the best ways to demonize their opponents."

Part of the strategy was to discredit the legitimacy of Congress; part of it was to discredit the mainstream media, and offer an alternative worldview, set of values and narratives via a range of new, conservative media. Fox News, Rush Limbaugh and other new conservative radio shows soon emerged.

Mann says it has troubled him, especially in the most recent presidential campaign, that journalists and commentators treated the two parties as though they both do the same thing, in roughly equal measure.

"Because the parties aren't the same, especially in this period. They've operated very differently. They have different value," he says. "It's the Republican Party that has really tried to weaken the institutions of government and to break the norms of our democratic system.

Mann says he and Ornstein have approached their work not as partisans but as scholars, looking at the evidence. He thinks more journalists and public commentators should do the same.

"We believe the public was disserved by emphasizing the importance of equivalence and treatment that doesn't mean you treat one fairly and the other unfairly," he says. "It means you treat them both fairly and honestly. And if there are real important consequential asymmetries between the parties, then, you'd do well to speak up."

The problem is, Mann says, the strategy that Gingrich outlined almost 40 years ago, to undermine trust in democratic institutions, has worked so well that many Americans no longer know who or what to believe.

People have separated on tribal grounds, with strong social, cultural and partisan identities, and they tend to believe what they hear from their own echo chamber and reject everything else," he says. "The problem is less in the stimulus, because we've always had disputes that had lots of lies and untruths in them. But you hoped over time there were at least enough ordinary citizens out there who would be moved by just sort of practical evidence and logical reasoning, and come up with the right thing. But now we see it's too tribal for that to happen. And that creates opportunities for very different kind of forces to operate in a democracy."

America's democracy has been tested and has proven resilient in the past, albeit with significant rough patches—the Civil War, the McCarthy Hearings, Jim Crow laws. Historians may look back on this era as another of those rough patches. Or it could turn out to be a different kind of era altogether.

"You know, populist movements have succeeded in changing democracies into autocracies all around the world," Mann says. "And it all starts with a successful election. And these are not coups or revolutions. And it seems to me one of the jobs and what I will be working on over this next year is trying to develop indicators and signs of what's illegitimate in American democracy and where it's appearing. And it's time for using public shame on such things and riling up people about the right kind of issues and it won't be easy. But I think it's going to take a more vigilant public. Obviously some people are not at all engaged in politics and don't care about it. The hope is there's enough of a more attentive activists concern segment of the public that can be active and in so doing help preserve a democratic system that's carried us 240 years."

Republicans and Democrats Are More Ideologically Divided Than Ever Before

Pew Research Center

The Pew Research Center is a nonpartisan think tank that analyzes, researches, and conducts polls related to domestic and global issues.

Republicans and Democrats are more divided along ideological lines—and partisan antipathy is deeper and more extensive—than at any point in the last two decades. These trends manifest themselves in myriad ways, both in politics and in everyday life. And a new survey of 10,000 adults nationwide finds that these divisions are greatest among those who are the most engaged and active in the political process.

The overall share of Americans who express consistently conservative or consistently liberal opinions has doubled over the past two decades from 10% to 21%. And ideological thinking is now much more closely aligned with partisanship than in the past. As a result, ideological overlap between the two parties has diminished: Today, 92% of Republicans are to the right of the median Democrat, and 94% of Democrats are to the left of the median Republican.

Partisan animosity has increased substantially over the same period. In each party, the share with a highly negative view of the opposing party has more than doubled since 1994. Most of these intense partisans believe the opposing party's policies "are so misguided that they threaten the nation's well-being."

"Ideological silos" are now common on both the left and right. People with down-the-line ideological positions—especially conservatives—are more likely than others to say that most of their close friends share their political views. Liberals and conservatives disagree over where they want to live, the kind of people they

"Political Polarization in the American Public," Pew Research Center, June 12, 2014. Reprinted by Permission.

want to live around and even whom they would welcome into their families.

And at a time of increasing gridlock on Capitol Hill, many on both the left and the right think the outcome of political negotiations between Obama and Republican leaders should be that their side gets more of what it wants.

These sentiments are not shared by all—or even most—Americans. The majority do not have uniformly conservative or liberal views. Most do not see either party as a threat to the nation. And more believe their representatives in government should meet halfway to resolve contentious disputes rather than hold out for more of what they want.

Yet many of those in the center remain on the edges of the political playing field, relatively distant and disengaged, while the most ideologically oriented and politically rancorous Americans make their voices heard through greater participation in every stage of the political process.

The rise of ideological uniformity has been much more pronounced among those who are the most politically active. Today, almost four-in-ten (38%) politically engaged Democrats are consistent liberals, up from just 8% in 1994. The change among Republicans since then appears less dramatic—33% express consistently conservative views, up from 23% in the midst of the 1994 "Republican Revolution." But a decade ago, just 10% of politically engaged Republicans had across-the-board conservative attitudes.

On measure after measure—whether primary voting, writing letters to officials, volunteering for or donating to a campaign—the most politically polarized are more actively involved in politics, amplifying the voices that are the least willing to see the parties meet each other halfway.

These are among the findings of the largest study of U.S. political attitudes ever undertaken by the Pew Research Center. Data are drawn from a national telephone survey of 10,013 adults, conducted from January through March of this year, and an ongoing series of follow-up surveys. This rich dataset, coupled with trends and insights from two decades of Pew Research Center polling, reveals a complex picture of partisan polarization and how it manifests itself in political behaviors, policy debates, election dynamics and everyday life.

What Polarization Looks Like

To chart the progression of ideological thinking, responses to 10 political values questions asked on multiple Pew Research surveys since 1994 have been combined to create a measure of ideological consistency. Over the past twenty years, the number of Americans in the "tails" of this ideological distribution has doubled from 10% to 21%. Meanwhile, the center has shrunk: 39% currently take a roughly equal number of liberal and conservative positions. That is down from about half (49%) of the public in surveys conducted in 1994 and 2004.

And this shift represents both Democrats moving to the left and Republicans moving to the right, with less and less overlap between the parties. Today, 92% of Republicans are to the right of the median (middle) Democrat, compared with 64% twenty years ago. And 94% of Democrats are to the left of the median Republican, up from 70% in 1994.

More Negative Views of the Opposing Party

Beyond the rise in ideological consistency, another major element in polarization has been the growing contempt that many Republicans and Democrats have for the opposing party. To be sure, disliking the other party is nothing new in politics. But today, these sentiments are broader and deeper than in the recent past.

In 1994, hardly a time of amicable partisan relations, a majority of Republicans had unfavorable impressions of the Democratic Party, but just 17% had *very* unfavorable opinions. Similarly, while most Democrats viewed the GOP unfavorably, just 16% had *very* unfavorable views. Since then, highly negative views have more than doubled: 43% of Republicans and 38% of Democrats now view the opposite party in strongly negative terms.

Even these numbers tell only part of the story. Those who have a very unfavorable impression of each party were asked: "Would you say the party's policies are so misguided that they threaten the nation's well-being, or wouldn't you go that far?" Most who were asked the question said yes, they would go that far. Among all Democrats, 27% say the GOP is a threat to the well-being of the country. That figure is even higher among Republicans, 36% of whom think Democratic policies threaten the nation.

Politics Gets Personal

Liberals and conservatives share a passion for politics. They are far more likely than those with more mixed ideological views to discuss politics on a weekly or daily basis. But for many, particularly on the right, those conversations may not include much in the way of opposing opinions.

Nearly two-thirds (63%) of consistent conservatives and about half (49%) of consistent liberals say most of their close friends share their political views. Among those with mixed ideological values, just 25% say the same. People on the right and left also are more likely to say it is important to them to live in a place where most people share their political views, though again, that desire is more widespread on the right (50%) than on the left (35%).

And while few Americans overall go so far as to voice disappointment with the prospect of a family member marrying a Democrat (8%) or a Republican (9%), that sentiment is not uncommon on the left or the right. Three-out-of-ten (30%) consistent conservatives say they would be unhappy if an immediate family member married a Democrat and about a quarter (23%) of across-the-board liberals say the same about the prospect of a Republican in-law.

To be sure, there are areas of consensus. Most Americans, regardless of their ideological preferences, value communities in which they would live close to extended family and high-quality schools. But far more liberals than conservatives think it is important that a community have racial and ethnic diversity (76% vs. 20%). At the same time, conservatives are more likely than liberals to attach importance to living in a place where many people share their religious faith (57% vs. 17% of liberals).

And the differences between right and left go beyond disagreements over politics, friends and neighbors. If they could choose anywhere to live, three-quarters of consistent conservatives prefer a community where "the houses are larger and farther apart, but schools, stores, and restaurants are several miles away." The preferences of consistent liberals are almost the exact inverse, with 77% saying they'd chose to live where "the houses are smaller and closer to each other, but schools, stores, and restaurants are within walking distance."

Polarization's Consequences

When they look at a political system in which little seems to get done, most Americans in the center of the electorate think that Obama and Republican leaders should simply meet each other halfway in addressing the issues facing the nation.

Yet an equitable deal is in the eye of the beholder, as both liberals and conservatives define the optimal political outcome as one in which their side gets more of what it wants. A majority of consistent conservatives (57%) say the ideal agreement between President Obama and congressional Republicans is one in which GOP leaders hold out for more of their goals. Consistent liberals take the opposite view: Their preferred terms (favored by 62%) end up closer to Obama's position than the GOP's.

Polarization in Red and Blue

The signs of political polarization are evident on both ends of the political spectrum, though the trajectory, nature and extent differ from left to right.

With Barack Obama in the White House, partisan antipathy is more pronounced among Republicans, especially consistently conservative Republicans. Overall, more Republicans than Democrats see the opposing party's policies as a threat and the differences are even greater when ideology is taken into account. Fully 66% of consistently conservative Republicans think the Democrats' policies threaten the nation's well-being. By comparison, half (50%) of consistently liberal Democrats say Republican policies jeopardize the nation's well-being. Conservatives also exhibit more partisan behavior in their personal lives; they are the most likely to have friends and prefer communities of like-minded people.

However, there is as much ideological uniformity on the left as the right. The share of Democrats holding consistently liberal views has grown steadily over the past 20 years, quadrupling from 5% in 1994 to 23% today. Social issues like homosexuality and immigration that once drove deep divides within the Democratic Party are now areas of relative consensus. And Democrats have become more uniformly critical of business and more supportive of government.

Changes in ideological consistency on the right have followed a different course. In 1994, during the "Republican Revolution," 13% of Republicans were consistent conservatives. That figure *fell* to 6% a decade later during George W. Bush's presidency, before rebounding to 20% today. This increase has come despite more moderate views among Republicans on issues like homosexuality and immigration, as GOP thinking on issues related to government and the economy has veered sharply to the right.

About the Study

This is the first report of a multi-part series based on a national survey of 10,013 adults nationwide, conducted January 23-March 16, 2014 by the Pew Research Center. The survey, funded in part through grants from the William and Flora Hewlett Foundation, the John D. and Catherine T. MacArthur Foundation and supported by the generosity of Don C. and Jeane M. Bertsch, is aimed at understanding the nature and scope of political polarization in the American public, and how it interrelates with government, society and people's personal lives.

The second report, coming in a few weeks, is the new Pew Research Center *Political Typology.* The typology – the sixth such study since 1987 – looks beyond Red vs. Blue divisions to gain a clearer understanding of the dynamic nature of the "center" of the American electorate, and the internal divides on both the left and the right.

Later, the project will explore the various factors that contribute to political polarization, or stem from it. A September report will examine how political polarization is linked to people's information environments: Their news sources, social media habits and interpersonal communication networks. Other reports will look at how political polarization relates to where people live, to their political environments, to how they view themselves and others around them, to their socioeconomic circumstances, to generational changes and to broader sociological and psychological personality traits.

The current report is divided into five parts: The first two focus on measuring the *nature and scope* of political polarization, emphasizing the difference between growing ideological consistency and rising partisan antipathy. The third looks closely at how polarization manifests itself in people's *personal lives.* The fourth looks at the relationship between polarization and *practical policymaking,* and the fifth digs deeper into how *political participation* both amplifies and reflects polarization.

About the Data

The data in this report are based on two independent survey administrations with the same randomly selected, nationally representative group of respondents. The first is the center's largest survey on domestic politics to date: the 2014 Political Polarization and Typology Survey, a national telephone survey of 10,013 adults, on landlines and cell phones, from January through March of this year. The second involved impaneling a subset of these respondents into the newly created American Trends Panel and following up with them via a survey conducted by web and telephone.

The Nation Can Come Together Following the 2016 Election

Jeff Singh

Jeff Singh is the writer, creator, and editor of AwakeFree.com, a site that addresses the personal, social, and global challenges of current times. He's also written for the Huffington Post.

Ever since Trump won a divisive presidential election, the battle lines are being drawn through cabinet selections, protests, the media and internet.

No matter where we turn, on our TVs, social media, and conversations, we are surrounded by political rhetoric.

How are we going to survive with our sanity to work together again and make progress as a nation?

For that matter, how are we going to survive the holidays? Cause, you know, everybody's got friends and relatives that are going to let you know how they feel.

While it's pointless to argue over fixed beliefs, we could instead, connect on deeper concerns.

Many have called for Trump, Hillary, and other leaders to step up and address the division earnestly.

Sigh, (deep breath). Seriously, take a deep breath right now.

We're not here to wait for leaders to dictate how we live our lives.

Reframing our own attitude and intent is the start of creating the change we want to see.

So here are 3 ways we can heal the divides, for our own sanity and the sanity of this nation.

1) Recognize the Problems

This is not some airy-fairy zone out of everything post.

So let's acknowledge the problems from a greater perspective.

First, the politicians or media are not paying you, are they? So why would your mind and voice be owned to repeat anyone else's rhetoric?

It's time to step back and think on your own again without those voices in your head.

For a moment, step out of attachment from a particular candidate or cause and see what's going on from both sides.

Understand, whenever you have people who feel disenfranchised, eventually you're going to have reactions. So far as people feel unheard, those reactions get louder and more aggressive. It's that simple, really.

In America these days, those on many sides of the political spectrum feel disenfranchised.

We've got to acknowledge the resentment of the silent majority in rural and industrial towns who voted for Trump to overthrow politics as usual—which was just not working for them, their jobs, or their security.

But it need not be at the hate and expense of women and minorities who really share the same concern for income equality and basic life security.

See, we have the same concerns for equality, security, and opportunity coming through different voices.

I wonder if you can recognize that we're fighting for the same basic needs from opposing sides. When we could rally around the same core issues—equality, security, opportunity.

Those core challenges are worth tackling together.

2) Connect With People Not Media

While it's certainly important to know what's going on in this crazy world, sometimes we can get over-saturated with updates.

Regardless if it's click-bait or fake news circulating social media, at least they got you to read and share. The advertisers thank you for your support.

While tragedies make headlines, what gets lost are stories of people helping people. These just don't rile up clicks like what Trump, Hillary, or the political pundits spin.

Just remember, regardless of political opinions, most people are still good and helpful. At least you are, right?

In New York City, you can't avoid different cultures and if you need directions, most anyone will help you out regardless of cultural backgrounds.

Listen, I grew up in the south, where if you got stuck on the road with a blown-out tire or needed a car battery charged, someone, perhaps in a pickup truck, would surely stop to help out even if they had radically different political opinions.

If we can get out of fear and resentment, back to those good ol' days of looking out for people, that's what would really "make America great again."

Perhaps sometimes it's good to take our noses out of media devices, and go out to have a conversation with friends. Heck, have conversations with people who may have different opinions. That's what holiday parties, cafés and bars are good for.

Let's just leave the argument-spinning to politicians and newsroom entertainers.

When we're not defending their agendas, we can get back to listening to each other again.

Sharing stories and concerns amiably, my friends, is how America is won back by the people.

3) Stand Up for People Not Politics

Since Trump won office, there's been a rise of bullying behavior from both sides.

The signs of hate are on the walls, along with a spike of harassment toward minorities, Trump trolls getting un-filtered on social media, and school children chanting, "build the wall" to Latino students.

Just as well, Trump protests turning into destructive riots are ridiculous.

As my friend would say, "ya'll done lost your mind?" You gotta keep that mind, cause you gonna need it for a few years.

Ultimately hateful talk or actions do nothing but polarize people deeper to defend their own opinions.

Of course there's anxiousness. If hate and bullying doesn't have you concerned, something's terribly wrong.

But there are more effective ways to get things done in this country.

One way to turn this around is to work in favor Of something rather than to hate something. Be a champion for people, for humanity, not against certain people.

There's a story about a guy who stood up to bank robbers. Even though he got shot 11 times, he managed to pull people out to safety. When asked why he did that over saving his own life, he simply responded, "It's what we do." He did not ask people he was saving about their opinions first. He just rescued people.

By standing up for each other, we overcome bullies on either side, simply because, "It's what we do."

Now Trump made a lot of promises to the working class for improving employment, building infrastructure and income equality.

If we can shake our heads out of blind acceptance, it behooves liberals and conservatives alike to monitor the situation and see how those promises hold up, to speak up for people when needed, to petition and peacefully protest when required.

We hired the political leaders into office. Let's ensure they work for us and we don't work for them.

Just Remember...

At the core we the people are really fighting for the same basic needs—equality, security, and opportunity. We may have different opinions and approaches, but that fundamental understanding can open up a more collaborative dialog.

We don't need to be sucking up to political leaders, with their own power games and agendas, or regurgitating media headlines to make a case.

Look at your own life, family, friends, and co-workers. What's more important here, political opinions or collaboration which really makes progress?

It's up to you what kind of country you want. It's up to you what you want to pass on to your children.

Your children could care less what political leaders have to say. But they do care what you have to teach them through your words and actions.

Regardless of politics, we can collaborate within our diversity for a greater America.

Perhaps that's the silver lining—getting woke up so we find our strength together.

It's Up to Us to Write a New Story After the Election

Charles Eisenstein

Charles Eisenstein is a teacher, speaker, and writer who focuses on themes of civilization, consciousness, money, and human cultural evolution.

Normal is coming unhinged. For the last eight years it has been possible for most people (at least in the relatively privileged classes) to believe that society is sound, that the system, though creaky, basically works, and that the progressive deterioration of everything from ecology to economy is a temporary deviation from the evolutionary imperative of progress.

A Clinton Presidency would have offered four more years of that pretense. A woman President following a black President would have meant to many that things are getting better. It would have obscured the reality of continued neoliberal economics, imperial wars, and resource extraction behind a veil of faux-progressive feminism. Now that we have, in the words of my friend Kelly Brogan, rejected a wolf in sheep's clothing in favor of a wolf in wolf's clothing, that illusion will be impossible to maintain.

The wolf, Donald Trump (and I'm not sure he'd be offended by that moniker) will not provide the usual sugarcoating on the poison pills the policy elites have foisted on us for the last forty years. The prison-industrial complex, the endless wars, the surveillance state, the pipelines, the nuclear weapons expansion were easier for liberals to swallow when they came with a dose, albeit grudging, of LGBTQ rights under an African-American President.

I am willing to suspend my judgement of Trump and (very skeptically) hold the possibility that he will disrupt the elite policy consensus of free trade and military confrontation—major themes of his campaign. One might always hope for miracles. However, because he apparently lacks any robust political ideology of his own, it is more likely that he will fill his cabinet with neocon war hawks, Wall Street insiders, and corporate reavers, trampling the wellbeing of the working class whites who elected him while providing them their own sugar-coating of social conservatism.

The social and environmental horrors likely to be committed under President Trump are likely to incite massive civil disobedience and possibly disorder. For Clinton supporters, many of whom were halfhearted to begin with, the Trump administration could mark the end of their loyalty to our present institutions of government. For Trump supporters, the initial celebration will collide with gritty reality when Trump proves as unable or unwilling as his predecessors to challenge the entrenched systems that continually degrade their lives: global finance capital, the deep state, and their programming ideologies. Add to this the likelihood of a major economic crisis, and the public's frayed loyalty to the existing system could snap.

We are entering a time of great uncertainty. Institutions so enduring as to seem identical to reality itself may lose their legitimacy and dissolve. It may seem that the world is falling apart. For many, that process started on election night, when Trump's victory provoked incredulity, shock, even vertigo. "I can't believe this is happening!"

At such moments, it is a normal response to find someone to blame, as if identifying fault could restore the lost normality, and to lash out in anger. Hate and blame are convenient ways of making meaning out of a bewildering situation. Anyone who disputes the blame narrative may receive more hostility than the opponents themselves, as in wartime when pacifists are more reviled than the enemy.

Racism and misogyny are devastatingly real in this country, but to blame bigotry and sexism for voters' repudiation of the

Establishment is to deny the validity of their deep sense of betrayal and alienation. The vast majority of Trump voters were expressing extreme dissatisfaction with the system in the way most readily available to them. Millions of Obama voters voted for Trump (six states who went for Obama twice switched to Trump). Did they suddenly become racists in the last four years? The blame-the-racists (the fools, the yokels…) narrative generates a clear demarcation between good (us) and evil (them), but it does violence to the truth. It also obscures an important root of racism—anger displaced away from an oppressive system and its elites and onto other victims of that system. Finally, it employs the same dehumanization of the other that is the essence of racism and the precondition for war. Such is the cost of preserving a dying story. That is one reason why paroxysms of violence so often accompany a culture-defining story's demise.

The dissolution of the old order that is now officially in progress is going to intensify. That presents a tremendous opportunity and danger, because when normal falls apart the ensuing vacuum draws in formerly unthinkable ideas from the margins. Unthinkable ideas range from rounding up the Muslims in concentration camps, to dismantling the military-industrial complex and closing down overseas military bases. They range from nationwide stop-and-frisk to replacing criminal punishment with restorative justice. Anything becomes possible with the collapse of dominant institutions. When the animating force behind these new ideas is hate or fear, all manner of fascistic and totalitarian nightmares can ensue, whether enacted by existing powers or those that arise in revolution against them.

That is why, as we enter a period of intensifying disorder, it is important to introduce a different kind of force to animate the structures that might appear after the old ones crumble. I would call it love if it weren't for the risk of triggering your New Age bullshit detector, and besides, how does one practically bring love into the world in the realm of politics? So let's start with empathy. Politically, empathy is akin to solidarity, born of the understanding that we are all in this together. In what together? For starters, we are in the uncertainty together.

We are exiting an old story that explained to us the way of the world and our place in it. Some may cling to it all the more desperately as it dissolves, looking perhaps to Donald Trump to restore it, but their savior has not the power to bring back the dead. Neither would Clinton have been able to preserve America as we'd known it for too much longer. We as a society are entering a space between stories, in which everything that had seemed so real, true, right, and permanent comes into doubt. For a while, segments of society have remained insulated from this breakdown (whether by fortune, talent, or privilege), living in a bubble as the containing economic and ecological systems deteriorate. But not for much longer. Not even the elites are immune to this doubt. They grasp at straws of past glories and obsolete strategies; they create perfunctory and unconvincing shibboleths (Putin!), wandering aimlessly from "doctrine" to "doctrine"—and they have no idea what to do. Their haplessness and half-heartedness was plain to see in this election, their disbelief in their own propaganda, their cynicism. When even the custodians of the story no longer believe the story, you know its days are numbered. It is a shell with no engine, running on habit and momentum.

We are entering a space between stories. After various retrograde versions of a new story rise and fall and we enter a period of true unknowing, an authentic next story will emerge. What would it take for it to embody love, compassion, and interbeing? I see its lineaments in those marginal structures and practices that we call holistic, alternative, regenerative, and restorative. All of them source from empathy, the result of the compassionate inquiry: What is it like to be you?

It is time now to bring this question and the empathy it arouses into our political discourse as a new animating force. If you are appalled at the election outcome and feel the call of hate, perhaps try asking yourself, "What is it like to be a Trump supporter?" Ask it not with a patronizing condescension, but for real, looking underneath the caricature of misogynist and bigot to find the real person.

Even if the person you face IS a misogynist or bigot, ask, "Is this who they are, really?" Ask what confluence of circumstances, social, economic, and biographical, may have brought them there. You may still not know how to engage them, but at least you will not be on the warpath automatically. We hate what we fear, and we fear what we do not know. So let's stop making our opponents invisible behind a caricature of evil.

We've got to stop acting out hate. I see no less of it in the liberal media than I do in the right-wing. It is just better disguised, hiding beneath pseudo-psychological epithets and dehumanizing ideological labels. Exercising it, we create more of it. What is beneath the hate? My acupuncturist Sarah Fields wrote to me, "Hate is just a bodyguard for grief. When people lose the hate, they are forced to deal with the pain beneath."

I think the pain beneath is fundamentally the same pain that animates misogyny and racism—hate in a different form. Please stop thinking you are better than these people! We are all victims of the same world-dominating machine, suffering different mutations of the same wound of separation. Something hurts in there. We live in a civilization that has robbed nearly all of us of deep community, intimate connection with nature, unconditional love, freedom to explore the kingdom of childhood, and so much more. The acute trauma endured by the incarcerated, the abused, the raped, the trafficked, the starved, the murdered, and the dispossessed does not exempt the perpetrators. They feel it in mirror image, adding damage to their souls atop the damage that compels them to violence. Thus it is that suicide is the leading cause of death in the U.S. military. Thus it is that addiction is rampant among the police. Thus it is that depression is epidemic in the upper middle class. We are all in this together.

Something hurts in there. Can you feel it? We are all in this together. One earth, one tribe, one people.

We have entertained teachings like these long enough in our spiritual retreats, meditations, and prayers. Can we take them now into the political world and create an eye of compassion inside the political hate vortex? It is time to do it, time to up our game. It is time to stop feeding hate. Next time you post on line, check your words to see if they smuggle in some form of hate: dehumanization, snark, belittling, derision.., some invitation to us versus them. Notice how it feels kind of good to do that, like getting a fix. And notice what hurts underneath, and how it doesn't feel good, not really. Maybe it is time to stop.

This does not mean to withdraw from political conversation, but to rewrite its vocabulary. It is to speak hard truths with love. It is to offer acute political analysis that doesn't carry the implicit message of "Aren't those people horrible?" Such analysis is rare. Usually, those evangelizing compassion do not write about politics, and sometimes they veer into passivity. We need to confront an unjust, ecocidal system. Each time we do we will receive an invitation to give in to the dark side and hate "the deplorables." We must not shy away from those confrontations. Instead, we can engage them empowered by the inner mantra that my friend Pancho Ramos-Stierle uses in confrontations with his jailers: "Brother, your soul is too beautiful to be doing this work." If we can stare hate in the face and never waver from that knowledge, we will access inexhaustible tools of creative engagement, and hold a compelling invitation to the haters to fulfill their beauty.

Organizations to Contact

The editors have compiled the following list of organizations concerned with the issues debated in this book. The descriptions are derived from materials provided by the organizations. All have publications or information available for interested readers. This list was compiled on the date of publication of the present volume; the information provided here may change. Be aware that many organizations take several weeks or longer to respond to inquiries, so allow as much time as possible.

The American Civil Liberties Union (ACLU)

125 Broad Street, 18th Floor
New York, NY 10004
(212) 549-2500
email: info@aclu.org
website: www.aclu.org

Founded in 1920, the ACLU is one of the nation's foremost defenders of civil liberties and the rights enshrined in the Constitution.

The Equal Justice Initiative

122 Commerce Street
Montgomery, AL 36104
(334) 269-1803
email: contact_us@eji.org
website: www.eji.org

The Equal Justice Initiative stands against social, racial, and economic injustices. It is working to end mass incarceration. EJI also provides legal aid.

**National Association for the Advancement
of Colored People (NAACP)**
4805 Mt. Hope Drive
Baltimore, MD 21215
(410) 580-5777
email: washingtonbureau@naacpnet.org
website: www.naacp.org

The NAACP works to eliminate race-based discrimination, whether it be educational, political, economic, or social.

Newseum
555 Pennsylvania Avenue NW
Washington, DC 20001
(202) 292-6100
website: www.newseum.org

The Newseum, which is located in Washington, DC, "explains and defends free expression and the five freedoms of the First Amendment: religion, speech, press, assembly and petition."

PEN America
588 Broadway, Suite 303
New York, NY 10012
(212) 334-1660
email: info@pen.org
website: www.pen.org

Pen America brings together writers and works to protect freedom of expression in the United States and around the world.

Pew Research Center
1615 L Street NW, Suite 800
Washington, DC 20036
(202) 419-4300
email: info@pewresearch.org
website: www.pewresearch.org

The Pew Research Center is a nonpartisan think tank that analyzes, researches, and conducts polls related to domestic and global issues.

Roosevelt Institute

570 Lexington Avenue, 5th Floor
New York, NY 10022
(212) 444-9130
email: info@rooseveltinstitute.org
website: www.rooseveltinstitute.org

The Roosevelt Institute brings together thought leaders from around the country to take on community issues and federal policies with the goal of "orienting toward a new economic and political system: one built by many for the good of all."

The Rutherford Institute

Post Office Box 7482
Charlottesville, VA 22906-7482
(434) 978-3888
email: staff@rutherford.org
website: www.rutherford.org

Based in Charlottesville, Virginia, the Rutherford Institute is a civil liberties nonprofit that provides legal services and conducts advocacy work. It was founded by John Whitehead, whose writing appears in this book.

The Southern Poverty Law Center

400 Washington Avenue
Montgomery, AL 36104
(334) 956-8200
email: https://www.splcenter.org/contact-us/general
website: www.splcenter.org

The Southern Poverty Law Center promotes social justice and equal opportunities. "Using litigation, education, and other forms of advocacy," the Southern Poverty Law Center "[fights] hate and bigotry and [seeks] justice for the most vulnerable members of our society."

United States House of Representatives
Washington, DC 20515
(202) 224-3121
website: https://www.house.gov/representatives/find

The United States House of Representatives is one of Congress's two chambers. The link above allows you to search for and contact your representative.

Bibliography

Books

Michelle Alexander, *The New Jim Crow*. New York, NY: The New Press, 2012.

Ta-Nehisi Coates, *Between the World and Me*. New York, NY: Spiegel & Grau, 2015.

Matthew Desmond, *Evicted: Poverty and Profit in the American City*. New York, NY: Broadway Books, 2016.

Thomas Frank, *Listen, Liberal: Or, What Ever Happened to the Party of the People?* New York, NY: Metropolitan Books, 2016.

Jacob Hacker and Paul Pierson, *American Amnesia: How the War on Government Led Us to Forget What Made America Prosper*. New York, NY: Simon & Schuster, 2015.

Chris Hayes, *A Colony in a Nation*. New York, NY: W. W. Norton & Company, 2017.

Arlie Hochschild, *Strangers in Their Own Land*. New York, NY: The New Press, 2016.

Nancy Isenberg, *White Trash: The 400-Year Untold History of Class in America*. New York, NY: Penguin Books, 2016.

Edward Luce, *The Retreat of Western Liberalism*. New York, NY: Atlantic Monthly Press, 2017.

Jane Mayer, *Dark Money: The Hidden History of the Billionaires Behind the Rise of the Radical Right*. New York, NY: Anchor, 2016.

George Packer, *The Unwinding: An Inner History of the New America*. New York, NY: Farrar, Straus and Giroux, 2013.

Claudia Rankine, *Citizen: An American Lyric*. Minneapolis, MN: Graywolf Press, 2014.

Richard Rothstein, *The Color of Law: A Forgotten History of How Our Government Segregated America*. New York, NY: Liveright, 2017.

J. D. Vance, *Hillbilly Elegy: A Memoir of a Family and Culture in Crisis*. New York, NY: Harper Collins, 2016.

Colin Woodward, *American Nations: A History of the Eleven Rival Regional Cultures of North America*. New York, NY: Penguin Books, 2012.

Periodicals and Internet Sources

Kurt Anderson, "How America Went Haywire," *Atlantic*, September 2017. www.theatlantic.com.

Ta-Nehisi Coates, "The Case for Reparations," *Atlantic*, June 2014. www.theatlantic.com.

Ta-Nehisi Coates, "My President Was Black," *Atlantic*, January 2017. www.theatlantic.com.

Arlie Russell Hochschild, "I Spent 5 Years With Some of Trump's Biggest Fans. Here's What They Won't Tell You," *Mother Jones*, September 2016. www.motherjones.com.

Charles A. Kupchan and Peter L. Trubowitz, "Grand Strategy for a Divided America," *Foreign Affairs,* July 2007. www.foreignaffairs.com.

Jeff Madrick, "America: The Forgotten Poor," *New York Review of Books*, June 22, 2017. www.nybooks.com.

Jane Mayer, "Covert Operations," *New Yorker,* August 30, 2010. www.newyorker.com.

New York Times, "Red, Blue and Divided: Six Views of America," *New York Times,* November 13, 2016. www.nytimes.com.

Evan Osnos, "The Fearful and the Frustrated," *New Yorker*, August 31, 2015. www.newyorker.com.

George Saunders, "Who Are All These Trump Supporters?," *New Yorker*, July 11, 2016. www.newyorker.com.

Sabrina Siddiqui, "Reporting While Muslim: How I Covered the US Presidential Election," *Guardian*, December 28, 2016. www.theguardian.com.

Andrew Sullivan, "America Is Still the Future," *New York*, January 2017. www.theatlantic.com.

Index

W

Y

Z